BONED
EVERY WHICH WAY

A Collection of Skeletal Literature
2019

Edited by
Nate Ragolia

SPACEBOY BOOKS

Denver, Colorado

Published in the United States by:

Spaceboy Books LLC
1627 Vine Street
Denver, CO 80206

www.readspaceboy.com

Content from BONED: bonedstories.wordpress.com

First printed May 2020

ISBN-13: 978-1-951393-89-2

Profits from sales of this book will benefit the Restaurant Employee Relief
Fund - rerf.us

For Diane Root—

Her brilliant words graced *BONED* early and often.
She will be dearly missed, and long remembered.

1939 - 2019

TABLE OF CONTENTS

THE PACKAGE
J. DAVID LISS

I

"There was a group of people sitting in a room. A package was delivered. They all left."

"Is that all we know, Jack?"

"That's it, detective."

"That's all he'll say?"

"Those are the only complete sentences he'll say. And he'll only answer questions that can be answered with a yes or no. Nothing more."

"What do you mean?"

"He can't answer open questions. If your questions aren't phrased to be answered either yes or no, he just stares at you and says nothing."

"Has Goldberg seen him?"

"Dr. Goldberg said to tell you that trauma does funny things to the mind and that it might take a while before the victim will be able to recount what happened. Right now, he'll only answer Yes/No questions."

"Then I don't know why the chief had to wake me up at 3:00 am to get on this case. It could have waited until 9:00." Of course, I did know why. Peter Hannon was the orthopedic surgeon for the mayor and for the Yankees. He was known as New York's top bone cutter. This would be in the newspapers. Anyway, the Chief likes waking me up early.

Being awake at 3:00 and needing little time to shower and dress, I searched for images and videos of Dr. Hannon. It wasn't hard to find them. He's a rock star. He's the surgeon that everyone said Mehmet Oz used to be like. Tall, slim, athletic, his silver hair and icy blue eyes inspired confidence. He moved his hands with coordinated grace when he gave speeches. Used to move his hands.

Jack continued, "Take a look at the guy. You'll be glad you haven't had breakfast. You know he was a surgeon? Looks like that's over with."

"I was briefed. Thanks for the heads up, though." The officer was Jack Dunne. He didn't have to warn me that the victim was mutilated and would be hard on the eyes. Many of the other cops wouldn't have bothered. Jack is a decent guy.

There was a group of people sitting in a room. A package was delivered. They all left.

That's what I had to work with. It reminded me of those existentialist one-act plays that were popular in the sixties, when every college student tried to be the next Sartre.

Actually, those plays were never popular except among a handful of English majors right before the munchies hit them.

I started formulating yes/no questions in my head as I walked into the ICU at the Hospital for Special Surgery. The ambulance had taken him to the hospital where he himself worked as a surgeon.

The Intensive Care Unit is a place that bounces between frenzy and stasis. But the ICU I walked into felt like neither. It felt like a battlefield right before the attack. People were looking for something to do, going through drug lists, checking machinery, reading patient records, anything to give themselves the sense that they were doing something.

But there was nothing for them to do. So the nurses and doctors stared at me as I came in and walked to Dr. Hannon's room, silently screaming "Stat" as I went passed.

"Dr. Hannon, I'm Detective Frank Scott from the 19th Precinct. Do you understand who I am?"

He looked at me with eyes that were pale blue and utterly lost.

"Yes."

Okay. My first Yes/No question came up affirmative. I was off to a good start.

"Doctor, do you know who did this to you?"

"Yes."

"Tell me who."

Silence. Lost stare. I knew that wasn't going to work but I wanted to see what would happen.

"Do you know why this was done to you?"

"There was a group of people sitting in a room. A package was delivered. They all left."

"Does that group of people have something to do with what happened to you?"

"Yes."

"Do you know who those people are?"

"Yes."

Do they know each other?"

"Yes."

"Were they together for a reason?"

"Yes."

"What was in the package?"

Silence. Stare.

"Do you know what was in the package?"

"Yes."

"Did the package contain your arm?"

"No."

The new round of anesthetics was starting to take hold. His eyes were closing. His doctor, standing next to me, said, "Detective, you'll have to leave and let Pete sleep. We'll call when he's awake and able to answer more questions. We all want you to solve this, to get the guys who did this to one of our best." As the doctor spoke, he was holding a scalpel, twisting it between his fingers.

I waited for the elevator and gave myself some time to indulge in self-pity. Some people in the precinct think that the brass always gives me the highest profile cases because I'm the smartest detective on the force. That's not it at all. I get the high-profile cases because I'm the most expendable detective on the force. I'm everybody's choice for the sacrificial lamb when something goes wrong on a case that's important to the mayor or another big shot. There's lots of reasons why. One: it was a mistake to raid the illegal gambling parlor in the garment district when Councilman Annunziato was there. How many years was I going to pay for that?

But that wasn't the real problem.

Of course, the real problem was my father.

So, I didn't get the high profile cases because I was smart. I got smart because I kept getting cases that could get me fired.

I went to get coffee and eggs, curse the chief, think of more binary questions. But I wasn't going to have breakfast alone. I called Daisy and suggested that she meet me at the Stanhope. The disadvantage of having my father is that the brass would boot me off the force in a second. The advantage is that I can have breakfast at the Stanhope every morning of the week if I wanted to, in spite of earning a detective's salary. I would buy Daisy's breakfast, not the department, which was one small reason she was willing to meet me. I don't tell Daisy anything. I suggest things to her that are in our mutual interest. After all, she is the Daily News' star crime reporter and I'm New York's own Sherlock Holmes, according to that august paper. Anyway, they do something at the Stanhope with bagels, smoked salmon, scrambled eggs and caviar that makes it worth getting up early.

II

It was about 1:00 pm when the on-duty officer called to let me know Dr. Hannon was alert enough for questioning. I chuckled to myself because I had just finished an early lunch and was in a good mood.

Usually these calls came right after I had ordered lunch and I had to leave before it was brought.

I could see in his pale, gated eyes that Hannon was in pain. But he wasn't pushing the button on the infusion pump to deliver more narcotic; he wanted to talk.

"Good afternoon doctor." Silence back.

"Are you ready for more questions?"

"Yes."

"Good. Were the people in the room gathered there for a common purpose?

"Yes. There was a group of people sitting in a room. A package was delivered. They all left."

"Was it to wait for the package they received?"

"Yes."

"Were they from the area or did they travel from far away?" Of course that got no answer. I tried again. Did these people travel from many places to be in that room?"

"Yes."

"Did it matter where they came from?"

"No."

"Did it matter what kind of room they were in?"

"No."

"Did they know what would be in the package?"

He didn't answer. I was confused. I had posed a yes/no question; he should have been able to answer it. Maybe he didn't know the answer. I thought of another approach.

"Did they believe they knew what was going to be in the package?"

He quickly answered, "Yes."

"Did they receive what they expected?" There was a pause and I thought that I would have to take another track when he hesitatingly answered, "No." He seemed confused.

What did hesitation mean?

"Do you know who the package was from?"

"Yes."

"Did the people waiting know who the package was from?"

"Yes."

"Was the package from you?"

"Yes," said Hannon in his flat and shell shocked voice, and he unconsciously inclined his head toward his ragged, bandaged shoulder where someone had hacked off his entire arm with what the forensic boys said was probably an ax. He looked like he was going to cry. Then his eyes got kind of blank and he stopped focusing on me. He was retreating.

Whatever it was, his mind wasn't ready to deal with it.

"Was the package a bomb or something else that could hurt the people in the room?"

"No."

"Detective, I'm going to have to ask you to stop questioning Dr. Hannon," said one of the residents. But I said, "I've been here for less than 20 minutes. I can't solve this case in 20-minute increments. I turned to Hannon.

"Dr. Hannon, please focus on me." I could see him struggle to stay with me. That kind of ability to concentrate is what made him a great surgeon. He was exerting his will."Dr. Hannon, did the people in the room have anything in common besides knowing each other?"

"Yes."

"Were they part of an organization of some kind?"

"No."

"Were they related?"

Silence.

I realized the term 'related' was too broad.

"Were they from the same family?"

"No."

"Did they meet for the first time in that room?"

"No."

"Does it matter where they first met?"

"Yes."

"Did they meet in a religious institution??

"No."

"A school?"

"No."

"Military service?"

"No."

I was getting desperate and blurted: "A boat, a plane, a train?"

"Yes."

He said yes.

"Which one?"

Silence.

"A boat?"

"No."

"A plane?"

"Yes."

They met on a plane.

But Hannon's eyes were closing now. He couldn't hold on any longer. The doctor said, "Detective Scott, time's up." I thanked him and left.

I needed to look up Dr. Hannon's travel itinerary.

III

I don't do forensic computing.

I can use e-mail. I search the Web. I have a Facebook page because the nine people I keep in touch with are on Facebook, though honestly I never look at it.

So I went to Matty, the geek that Central lends to the Precinct when we're on a high profile case. I think Matty's real name is Martin, not Matthew, but everyone calls him Matty because he doesn't shower much and his hair is usually kind of matted.

"Detective Scott! Looks like you're about to lose your job again. I hear this case involves the Mayor's barber."

"Matty, Dr. Hannon is a prominent surgeon at the Hospital for Special Surgery and he heals the Mayor's aching shoulder. But he's suffered a terrible accident and won't probably work again. So your genius is again required... don't hold out your hand to be shaken Matty. It just tells me you didn't wash your hands after taking a crap. Save the fecal coliforms for your keyboard."

"What makes you think I wipe my ass after crapping, Detective? That's the surest way to get your hands dirty. Now what can I find for you? The doctor's credit card history?"

"Travel history, Matt. Dr. Hannon was on an airplane and I want to know which one, where it went, and who was on the plane with him."

"What can you give me? Flight number? Airline? Dates?"

"None of the above Matt. If I had that, I wouldn't need a genius; I would simply need an app, or a bot, or a Trojan worm virus. But you will have to start with his name and find me the details."

Matt began searching. "Francis, it wasn't one of the commercial lines. If he flew in the last year, it must have been a private charter and that's going to take me more time. I'll have it for you tomorrow."

I believed he would. Matt boasted about his ability to substitute caffeine, sugar, and animal fat for sleep. He said he didn't sleep when his mind was engaged with work, and since, if rumor were true, he had no life outside of work, he would continue at his keyboard until he had an answer. Or died of the toxins in his own filth. Though he seemed immune to them, as well as to his own body odor.

"Use the cell to reach me. I won't be at my desk the next couple of days."

"Tomorrow," said Matt. "I won't call you in a couple of days. I'll call you tomorrow."

IV

I was having dinner with my father that night.

I always liked my dad. I liked him when he was Governor. I liked him when Maurice Brody, the NYC Police Commissioner became NYS Attorney General. I liked him when Brody led the crusade that sent my father to prison for six months on corruption charges. I liked my dad when, on the strength of prosecuting my father, Brody became the Governor. I liked dad when he got out of jail.

Then something interesting happened. All sorts of information about Brody, the sitting Governor, former Police Commissioner and AG, came out that made it clear he was spending public dollars on his own sex life. And it was an ugly sex life indeed. The Daily News never revealed who fed them the information that led to the story, which forced a prosecution that drove the Governor from office. The girls and boys who were abused by Brody brought criminal and civil charges against him. The criminal charges sent him to jail for three years and the civil charges cost him his wealth and his marriage. No one asked the question: how could these young people afford the kind of high-powered legal representation they brought to the court? Governor Brody became listed on the State's sex offender registry, where he remains to this day and probably always will, thanks to the law he himself signed making it almost impossible to get off.

My father did something that was completely out of character. He sent an e-mail to the shamed former Governor that said: I know exactly what you are going through, each step, each shame—the look in your wife's eye as she wonders how this can be, the shock in your children's faces as their world is overturned. As the cards were overturned, I empathized completely with the dismay you must have felt as if I were there with you, watching each card turn face up.

Dad is not empathetic. And he rarely commits anything to writing. He said when the e-mail was reported, "I really felt like writing to sympathize with the man who ended my Governorship and lost his own." After that, I found I liked my father a little bit less.

There was no connection found between my father and anything that happened to Brody—and believe me, the cops looked. Brody was a popular figure among law enforcement both for having served on the force and for always taking the position that the police were right, the accused wrong. Dad was a liberal. Brody a conservative. Brody Sees Blue was the saying on the force.

But that e-mail hung out like a bright red warning light and there wasn't a cop in the City who didn't think my father wasn't responsible for Brody's downfall. I became the most unpopular man on the force and would have lost my job four years ago if I hadn't been the only detective who was able to solve the New Legend murders. That was a public triumph for the Department and I became a citywide hero. The News, which must have figured it owed one to the family (though there was no connection to the Brody story, of course) made me out to be a bigger hero than I should have been. I became hard to fire. For the last four years, the Department had been looking for a way to make it easier in the form of really hard cases. That was a double-edged sword. If I failed, I failed in a very public way. But when I succeed, it makes me the City's "Great Detective" and completely untouchable by the brass.

No, I don't need to work. Dad made his money before he was Governor, and paying for lawyers did not come close to using it up. I just like being a detective. And I like hard cases.

My father follows the news closely, particularly anything that has to do with me. "That's quite a case you're on, Frank. I met Dr. Hannon a number of years ago when we awarded the money for the genomic institute on the East Side. He was very compelling. Any idea on what happened?"

"Can't talk about the case, Dad. Meaning no."

It was a presidential election year and because there were tight races in both party primaries, the New York primary elections had the unusual circumstance of actually mattering. In such a year, it was almost impossible to get my father to speak about anything except politics, and that used up much of our night.

As I was getting ready to leave, my father said, "About that case. One thing I remember about Hannon. When he accepted the money for the institute as part of a coalition of hospitals and research centers, he made it all about himself. On a stage full of very big egos, he managed to make sure everyone in the crowd, including Governor Me, knew or believed it was his project. He seemed above it all. But nobody is above it all; I know that better than anyone. I felt glad he was a surgeon and not a politician, because sure as anything that physician is a Republican."

My father always has such interesting insights.

V

The City garbage trucks were banging cans outside my 14th floor window at 6:00 that morning, and with the same predictability my cell phone was carrying Matty's scratchy voice to my irritated ear.

"While you were sleeping Francis, I was working and have some really, really good shit for you. Last year Hannon was on one of those high-priced adventure charters that was going to the Aleutian Islands in the spring for a month of pretend scientific shit. They don't really do science on those trips. It's really about having a luxury vacation in a setting that these rich bastards can be the first to spoil. You may have been on one or two of those.

"The plane crashed and the 14 passengers were lost. Coast Guard searched for three weeks before they were found."

"How is that possible, Matty? I would have heard about a plane of big shots going down."

"That's what makes this so unusual. The tour company was the exclusive Cecil Bradford Travel. I don't know why, but they paid a fortune to hush this up. I don't mean just to lawyers and flacks. I saw millions of dollars transferred to the accounts of the individual

---

passengers in a very quiet way. Using a bunch of dummy accounts, CBT paid off what must have been half their corporate treasury to those passengers. Furthermore, they never put in an insurance claim. They just paid."

"What were they hiding?"

"Don't know. Couldn't find any paper trail. Not a single e-mail. It's like listening to a choir of lawyers performing the famous melody, "Ain't Nobody Here Gonna Sing"—nobody's making a sound. I was able to see a huge jump in phone calls but couldn't get any content. Whatever they were paying to keep quiet, they got their money's worth. But here's another interesting thing. Only one of the 14 passengers did not get a dime. Wanna guess which one? Fuck, I'll tell ya. It was Hannon."

"My, my. Matty, that is interesting. Send me the passenger manifest. Was there anybody we know on board?"

"No one we've dealt with. There's a guy with a disturbing psych background. Lot's of treatment because the docs think he could be dangerous, but absolutely no criminal record. Apparently the nut job has no conscience, but no initiative either."

"Hmm. While we're breaking into Protected Health Information, were there any medical expenditures for those passengers after they returned?"

"Wait just a few minutes." I waited about 10 minutes while Matty grunted and clicked his fingers. "Here we go. No insurance claims. They must have been healthy when they returned to civilization."

"Or well taken care of."

"Meaning?"

"It just seems like everything was taken care of when they got back. I have a question that I need answered and I don't know if it can be found in the passenger health insurance claims. In the past year, have these individuals changed their doctors? Is that something you can check?"

"I told you: no insurance claims."

"Did any of them have their driver's license revoked?"

"That will take me a couple of hours to check, Francis. I'm going to have to hack into the DMV records in at least seven states. What am I looking for?"

"Not sure."

"Yes you are. You're just not talking."

"Thank you Matty. This is good stuff."

VI

The Daily News had scooped the other NY rags on the case and had blasted it on the front page. By today, the Post had followed suit. It was the only thing playing on the local TV and radio stations. The NY Times had put it on the front page of the Metro Section. But this case was national news fodder; it was too spectacular. NYPD's Deputy Commissioner for Public Affairs, Mickey Moran, was in his total glory, which meant that the was cursing his head off, blaming me for the apocalypse, chain smoking in the office against the rules of God, man and Mayor, demanding that I get fired, and begging me to do media interviews.

He spoke softly. "Nice of you to come to the fucking office, Sherlock. I guess that long, luxurious morning shower takes time. You do need to be well coiffed if you're going to talk to the ladies and gentlemen of the press." Then at the top of his lungs: "How often do I have to tell you not to talk to the media! You solve the fucking crime; I deal with the reporters. It's called 'division of labor.' Is that so hard for a genius like you?"

"Good morning Deputy Commissioner. I hope and pray that you are protecting me from the rapacious New York media."

"Oh, this goes well beyond the New York media, Frank. Forensic Files, The First 48, Dateline NBC, I got fucking Lester Holt and Anne Curry calling. I got John Walsh calling. I got the fucking Journal of the fucking American Medical Association calling about the fair-haired Doctor Hannon. You've really stirred the shit with this one."

"I didn't chop his arm off, Mickey. I'm trying to figure out who chopped his arm off. You've got role confusion again."

"Enough shit, detective. I'm going to need three hours today for interviews."

"Once again you exhibit role reversal syndrome. I think you should spend some time with Dr. Goldberg. Mickey, it's your job to talk to the media. I'm working the case. None of these guys want to tell the story unless they know the ending. Tell them you'll call when we know how it ends. I'm not talking to reporters today." That wasn't entirely true. I might have dinner with Daisy. First though, I would stop off at the hospital and see if I could make more progress with Hannon. I had two questions I wanted to ask him.

VII

No one expects trouble on sunny mornings. I showed my badge at the security desk in the front lobby, though the guards knew who I was. Why antagonize anyone? Reporters were waiting outside the front of the hospital, but Security didn't let them past the front door, so once I was in, it was nice and quiet. I took the elevator to the fourth floor, to the ICU.

I stepped off the elevator as a blast came screaming through the unit like a siren without its ambulance. An alarm went off. A tensed-up man's voice said over the loudspeakers with too much amplification, "Code Black. Alert. Code Black. Fourth floor ICU, Code Black." I was on the fourth floor ICU. Code Black. That meant an intruder was in the hospital. I ran to Hannon's room and suddenly it seemed like half the hospital was doing the same.

Hannon's door was closed. On the floor in front of the door was a cop, collapsed, covered in blood, spurting blood from the right back side of his head. It was Jack Dunne.

The stat team was already there with a crash cart. I stepped past them and opened the door. Hannon was in his room looking terrified. He was unharmed. I didn't know if Jack was going to live, but he did his job, he protected Hannon. Before he hit the floor, he sounded his alarm. I could hear the sirens of the squad cars arriving. Hospital security were all over the floor. I had no doubt that whoever attacked Jack had disappeared in the confusion, but whoever it was never got passed the closed door into Hannon's room.

Jack was one of the smartest cops on the force. I would have bet money that no one could sneak up on him when he was on guard. But someone did and hit him on the head with something hard and blunt.

Everyone's attention was focused on Jack. I walked over to Hannon and spoke to him very quietly, almost directly into his ear. "Dr. Hannon, I need you to focus on me. Focus!" He turned and looked at me. "I am going to ask you only two questions. I think we can solve this case, but I need you to stay with me and focus. Are you ready?"

"Yes."

"Did the people waiting in the room all have only one arm?"

"Yes."

"Were their arms removed with great surgical skill under very difficult conditions?"

His answer was the single word that I expected. How could one, small word be so infused with pride, shame, sorrow, triumph?

I learned later that they did save Jack's life, though he was in no shape to serve on the force after that and left on disability. I still see him now and then when I visit the deli he owns with his wife and brother-in-law.

VIII

It was two days later and Matty had delivered. I was ready to solve the case in a way that would make it ever harder for the Commissioner to fire me, and frankly, that meant high drama. The brass hated my sense of drama.

"Good morning, Dr. Hannon."

No answer. The stenographer and videographer were prepared to capture his answers, simple as they may be. The psychiatrist Dr. Goldberg was there too.

"Are you ready for more questions?"

"Yes."

"Were the people waiting in the room your fellow passengers from the lost CBT Flight 590 to the Aleutian Islands?"

"Yes."

"Were you in the room with them?"

"No."

"Were they expecting you?"

"No."

"But they were expecting the package from you?"

"Yes."

"Did they believe the package was going to be your left arm?"

"Yes."

"But it wasn't, was it?"

"No."

"Was it an arm that you removed from one of the patients at the hospital who had come in for the purpose of having it removed?"

"Yes."

"Did your fellow passengers think it was your arm?"

"Yes."

"Did you tell them it was your arm?"

"Yes."

"Dr. Hannon, I will tell you what I think happened to your arm and to the passengers of Flight 590. At any point, you can interrupt me and say 'yes,' or 'no.' When I'm finished, if I got it right, please say 'yes.' If I'm wrong, please say 'no.' Do you understand?"

"Yes."

"When the flight crashed in the Northern Atlantic, you all thought it was the end. You were woefully unprepared because you expected to reach the Aleutians and be treated like royalty at a resort hotel. You all felt lucky that the plane landed in the ocean right next to one of the smaller Islands and everyone made it to shore except the pilots.

"But it didn't take long for you all to get hungry. Things got desperate. Help seemed distant. Then you had a suggestion. You, an orthopedic surgeon, would remove everyone's arm of least use. The order in which the passengers would give up their arms would be determined by drawing lots. Only you would be exempted for the obvious reason that you needed both hands to perform the surgery. Hopefully, help would come before everyone had to sacrifice a limb. But it didn't. So one passenger at a time, you surgically removed everyone's non-dominant arm. And you all shared the protein along with anything else that was edible on the island until you were rescued.

"But you weren't going to be let off the hook. You agreed to have your arm removed if you ever made it back to civilization. And you did get back and realized at that moment what kind of Devil's bargain you had made. It's not just the disfigurement. You would never be able to work again. You would not be able to save lives. It was wrong.

"So you corresponded with the others and told them you had the surgery done and were having trouble with the recovery. You instructed them to meet in a hotel room in LaGuardia Airport and you would have the arm delivered so they could see it.

"Somehow, someone figured out that the package didn't contain your arm. And they came after you and did this to you.

"Am I right?"

There were tears in Hannon's eyes, falling silently, unwiped.

"It was Newark Airport."

"Dr. Hannon, you're speaking!"

"It was Newark. They met at Newark Airport, not LaGuardia. Otherwise you got it right. I actually thought about having my arm removed, but none of my colleagues was willing to remove a healthy arm, especially not mine."

"You were attacked by two of the passengers who figured out it wasn't your arm, and they mutilated you. One of them was Reinhold Biner, correct?"

"Yes. He was insane and would do anything Patricia Niesmith asked." Hannon started to cry for real. "When they realized that I hadn't sent my own arm, they wanted revenge." Hannon was totally losing it now; he was getting hysterical. "Biner cut off my arm with an ax."

"I wondered how they were able to sneak up on Jack Dunne. But if he saw two people missing arms, he would have assumed they were patients. After all, this is the Hospital for Special Surgery. So he turned his back on them."

I had to ask a final question. "Dr. Hannon, how did Niesmith know it wasn't your arm?"

"There was a band of pale skin around the ring finger. The arm had belonged to someone who was married and wore a ring long enough that his ring finger had a permanent, white band. I've been divorced for years. Patty knew that. We came from the same circle here on the Upper East Side. Had even dated for a while. She is unstable; I saw that when we dated twenty years ago. When we met to train for the trip, the first thing she had done was look at my left hand and note that I was no longer married."

"Doctor, you'll be pleased to know that Biner has already been picked up. I'm putting out an All-Points Bulletin for Niesmith. We'll have her soon."

Her picture in The Daily News would also help us catch her. Just behind a doorway to the room we were in, Daisy Stein, was scribbling away. I think it must have been she who had called the newspaper and told them to find a picture of Patricia Niesmith for the front cover. I wonder if my name would be in the headline. Couldn't wait to see the Chief's face.

In 1984 J. David Liss received an MFA from Brooklyn College. Trained in writing, inclined to politics, he worked as a speechwriter and lobbyist for causes that allow him to earn a living but are worthwhile. Liss published poetry and fiction in a number of places, including a recent anthology from Between the Lines Press.

A HALF-SECOND AGO, I SAW THAT THAT WASN'T
J. PIERCE

I was two people, a handwritten note hung from a chair in a store:
Do not sit. There wasn't a chair in the room, only
what was there. What was there wasn't; wasn't, was.

Oh, God, I don't want to bullshit you: If you wake up, you will see

snow.

Poems of J. Pierce have most recently appeared or are forthcoming in Thin Air Magazine, Packingtown Review, and Triggerfish Critical Review. One chapbook, Still Life with Rotting Baseball, was published by High5 Press.

RADIO SKULL TRANSMISSION
ANDREW SPENCE

The radio tower blinks with life.

I have control.

I am on its wavelength.

A 50 foot metal skeleton,
feels like narcissism.

my wired tendon
is attracted to the buzz,

the electricity

of flesh in a microwave

The bubble lighted fried squirrel
climbed too high
on me
now tiny
an electric scarecrow.

pain from commercial breaks
pulses out my eye sockets
electric animals scratch at my face
tear the flesh tender
like yellow-tail cheek bones

fluoride white-wash
my jaw
cracks the largest smile
gums hang,
ooze,

drip,

then screeches into the wind
and
leaves me fried

Smiling bone teeth

on the red blinking radio tower
I'm all skull smiles
Croaking out laughter

Andrew Spence is a broken hurricane of nonsense waiting to crash onto the beach of your boredom. 25 years old and currently residing in Denver, Colorado, Spence first grew up in Midwestern Ohio suburbia before he fell in love with mountain hikes. Recently graduated in the fields of Asian Studies and English Education, Andrew's poems often reflect his experiences abroad intermingled between the beautiful and sometimes disturbing images of being a lifelong learner in a world so quick to teach him a lesson. Andrew makes a hobby out of poetry, skateboards, alcohol and book collecting. He knows very well that he wouldn't be anywhere without his monthly calendar with pictures of basset hounds and late night long-board rides full of self-loathing.

THE PIANIST
RENTON THORNE

It began where it stopped –
The anorexic abhorrence of eating;
The definition of the ribcage
With nutrition-lack increasing.

He began to starve himself
Until his bones turned into keys.
The only thing he ate was Beethoven
In lonely moments such as these.

Starved himself to life in death
And overindulged in the famish;
Starved himself until his breath
Began to wither away and vanish.

Only in the end did he rejoice
When he was nothing left
But dust and warts.
He played: "No one would hear my voice,
But maybe they'll listen to my corpse."

Renton Thorne, born in Colorado, having lived in Missouri, Texas, Montana, Arkansas, California, and Massachusetts, has always loved American vernacular and the gritty American poetry of the 20th and 21st centuries. Recently graduating from Suffolk University, he now turns his full attention to getting his poetry published.

BEAUTIFUL BONES
DIANE ROOT

He liked her best near the window in the living room where she always sat. The changing light seemed to make her glow; from pale pink to gold, from sunset oranges and fiery reds, from lavender to the blanched blue of moonlight.

He loved to dress her almost even more. Silks, shimmering shantung and satins, taffetas and tweeds, lace, linens and leather—saris and sarongs, dashikis and dresses, huipils and wide-brimmed hats. A master chemist and a consummate chess player, he traveled the world, never failing to bring back native dress and fabrics in which to dress her.

Her passion for him knew no bounds. She did whatever he asked, so when he suggested that she lose weight, she complied without hesitation. Indeed, the thinner she became, the greater his "love" for her and the more passionate their lovemaking. Once described as an Auguste Renoir, rounded and lush, she became an Egon Schiller. She was soon a body of nearly bare bones, purposely self-starved with his help in order to keep him in thrall.

He, too, complied with this regime, since, after all, he had instigated it. He held up his side of the bargain, as well; if he barely fed her, he satisfied her passion that grew with every fleeting pound of flesh. As time passed, he became a more and more inventive lover, more and more obsessed with the end game.

But despite their amatory trysts, he did not think of her. He thought of her mother with whom he was really in love. Thinking of her, the final throes of passion became more acute, overwhelming for both of them. At the end, it didn't take long before the daughter died of passion. And starvation. A murder, without a murderer.

The Mother was more petite than her daughter ("She takes after her father," she said, clearly disgruntled).

Of French-Italian heritage, born in the South of France, the Mother was a delicately boned creature with a fierce and passionate character. Olive-skinned with sparkling bright ebony eyes that could flash love, lust, affection and anger in rapid succession should the situation require it—and even if it didn't. She was nothing if not mercurial.

Hers was the perfect body, just over five feet tall, delicately structured, but with beautiful ample breasts and rounded hips, she was feminine in all the right places. She was chic and very French. When she was still in her native country, married to her daughter's father, she was deemed to be one of France's most beautiful women of the day.

She spoke with a slight accent that somehow made her all the more fascinating. Then there was something else he could not quite put his finger on: she was somehow exotic. She was also as passionate as he was. For him. she was the perfect combination.

In comparison, her daughter couldn't hold a candle to her.

++++

They had already prepared the cellar with a bathtub, quickly filled with a potent flesh-eating acid. What little remained of her was promptly buried in the garden, soon much admired by the neighbors for its flowers sporting brilliant hues, especially zinnias, her favorites. Everything else vanished.

Everything, that is, except for her skeleton. They carried it upstairs, if somewhat gingerly, and placed it in her favorite chair by the window. They shrouded it for a decent interval in widow's weeds until the next day. ("She would doubtless mourn her passing," he said.) They even lit a few candles near her. They reveled in her beauty by the flickering light.

That night, they celebrated with champagne and caviar and candlelight. And passion. He had won his Queen. The daughter was only a pawn set up for slaughter.

Only later, did they delight in dressing her with the finery from foreign climes. "You know, she always did have beautiful bones," the Mother declared, "Just like mine."

And sometimes, when a spring day zephyr wafted through an open window or a winter wind whistled in winter, a soft rustle, a creak, then an almost inaudible rattle, a voice from afar perhaps, a mournful moan maybe, could be heard in their room.

Diane Root, a dual-national, was born in Paris of an American father, the journalist and writer, Waverley Root, and a French mother. Primarily known as a painter, she is, as she describes herself, "an accidental writer." She never sought to be published but that notwithstanding, she was nonetheless published in the New York Times Magazine ("The Artful Dodger" about lunch with Picasso) and various other venues. View her art: http://matakia.com.

BONES
NATALIE CRICK

I have to go back.
I have to keep searching

for something alive
among the dead.

I am yet undecided
how to arrange

her bones.
I want to conjure

the dark red throbbing heart.
Regrow her hair and teeth

the way they used to be.
Her legs are in my hands,

cool to the touch
like bottled milk.

Better, perhaps, to leave her alone,
unfeeling and without question.

Natalie Crick, from the UK, has poetry published or forthcoming in a range of journals and magazines in the UK including Interpreters House, Bare Fiction, Poetry Salzburg Review, Poetry Scotland, The SHOp and London Grip. Outside of the UK she has work published in Rust and Moth, The Chiron Review, 2River, The Ofi Press, The Perch Arts and Literary Magazine (Yale University), Plath Profiles, Red Paint Hill and The Adirondack Review. She is studying for an MA in Writing Poetry at Newcastle University (UK) and is currently taught by Tara Bergin and Jacob Polley. Her poetry has been nominated for the Pushcart Prize twice.

RAIN DANCE
G. ROE UPSHAW

What blithe requiescence there must've been
While Noah's world was being drowned:
A deluge expects nothing from nobody, and
Expects you to expect the same, cause
A downpour always dwindles. Then doors open,
Expectation pandiculates under a workaday rainbow,
Sending scrunched shoulders in their upturned collars
Through the mizzle on a two-hundred mile pilgrimage
To wound their gazes on my window, staring
At the queer boy tossing bones
Into a fire, wheeling and singing
Jealous junky pistol songs to stick up the sky,
To rob it of its rain.

G. Roe Upshaw is a sniveling, scribbling scrivener placed variously around the United States. He works tirelessly at his lyrics and his books, and works tiresomely at most everything else. He is honored to be included as a part of BONED.

COGITO ERO SUM
DIANE ROOT

In the beginning was the Word ...T.S. Eliot.

There was no doubt that he was not just handsome, but beautiful. The golden curly hair, a halo surrounding a sculptured head, seemingly perennially sunlit; the face of aquiline nose and sky-blue eyes, ever so slightly almond-shaped; the lithe body, flexible and fine-boned; the near-swan neck that rested on carved collar bones squarely set on broad, tanned shoulders; the swimmer's smooth torso, sculpted by the sea he so loved.

Sleek as a seal, he slipped effortlessly through the waves and into the deep. He would emerge, flashing a triumphant smile, casting off the sunlit droplet diamonds that quivered on his bronzed body that cascaded back onto the cool glittering aqua surface of a warm and foreign ocean.

There was no other way to describe it, as her friends would readily tell whoever might ask either then or later, she adored him. Not hard, they would say, to love an Adonis. A Piscean Adonis, which explained, she thought, for his love of all things finned and scaly. The more dangerous, the better. But that was the dark side—the side that nobody saw. Except her.

Clearly goldfish were not for him; too tame, he declared. No matter how fancy, koi, he joked, were too coy. Nor would sea horses do, a favorite among some of his diving buddies. "Too domesticated," he said. "The males carry and rear the young in their pouches. Can you imagine!" Unacceptable. He was nothing if not macho.

When he first acquired the aquarium, he had even considered barracudas—but soon rejected them as being too ugly. Piranhas, he finally decided, were "the real stuff." As for the subservient seahorses, the preference for piranhas made short work of that idea.

And "short work" was precisely what she wanted.

Besides, he liked his fish with serious teeth. Big, sharp teeth. Sharks were his favorites, but he decided to settle for what he could fit into a fair-sized aquarium.

Piranhas, in his mind, were the perfect solution. After all, they were not unlike scaled-down sharks. Those carnivorous, vicious specimens of the finned fleet held a special fascination for him. Needle-like dentition and a prehistoric past. In his view, they couldn't be more perfect.

Not long afterward, he had his heart's desire. Like others would refer to a pride of lions or a pod of whales, he referred to a [perfection?] passion of piranhas.

***

Her father had said: "The more brilliant the sun, the darker the shadow." She remembered that when she, a taxidermist and a chemist, had contemplated the brilliance of her husband's beauty for far too long, time no longer counted. The only thing that counted were the mistresses—the blonde bimbos, the red-haired hell-hath-no fury females, the raven-haired reticent mysterious ones—just to name a few. There were others, but by this time she had lost count. And by that time, it didn't matter. His fate was sealed, she chuckled, in more ways than one.

***

The shadow he cast was dark indeed, not that anyone was particularly aware of or even recognized its manifestation. Around there, people tended to mind their own business. Rumors only roamed in bars that no one ever admitted going to and as dark as the secrets they enclosed.

***

The devil-may-care golden boy had more devil than care. The darkness within inhabited him like an unseen shroud casting the deadly night shade of a poisonous tree. Devil, she suddenly realized, contained the real essence of his satanic side: the word *evil*.

Even Adonis's mother, a literate woman, said that. But nobody ever heard her, of course, since she had died mysteriously when he was just a boy in Florida. A boy who liked all things scaled, especially snakes—most particularly the colorful, banded ones—with a pretty name: corals. Skillful, even way back then, he caught one of them and draped it around her neck.

"Look how beautiful it is," he said. Right before the snake bit her.

***

She planned the bath carefully. It had to be inviting, his favorite color —the blue-green of tropical waters. A "foam bubble blanket," perhaps "chemically induced" to keep him "warm and playful" that would float and later hide what would be slipped into the water. Yes, that might do.

With her usual adoring solicitude, she oiled and perfumed her hands and his body with an elixir of attar of roses from Morocco. She slid her hands everywhere, even over his most intimate parts, eliciting ecstasy from him; low and melodic, he moaned, gradually reaching the higher pitch of release, satisfied at last. Later, she left him still in the bath lit by honey-scented candles with a glass of champagne. A special champagne, one laced with drops of ergot. *Cogito, ergot sum*, she thought.

She liked playing with words.

As handsome as he was, she too was quite beautiful. Lithe and long-limbed, she walked like a ballet dancer. The unsmiling cool ivory oval face reminded anyone who beheld her of a Modigliani. The graceful arms and hands, usually still at her sides or on her lap, now stealthily introduced a new element into the bath as, slightly somnolent, his head slowly began to sink beneath the blue water.

It was then, and only then, that she tipped the contents of the aquarium into the bath.

***

It didn't take long.

The first screeches slithered within her hearing and slid into her heart, now as ecstatic as his had been only moments before.

The excruciating screams slivered into shrieks, streaking and slicing the air with screeches, jagged and angular, sharp as knives, dissecting the dusk, cutting into the corners, shattering–at last–like glass.

Then, and only then, the ensuing silence, as strident as his cries, slipped silken into her soul, did she smile.

Diane Root, a dual-national, was born in Paris of an American father, the journalist and writer, Waverley Root, and a French mother. Primarily known as a painter, she is, as she describes herself, "an accidental writer." She never sought to be published but that notwithstanding, she was nonetheless published in the New York Times Magazine ("The Artful Dodger" about lunch with Picasso) and various other venues. View her art: http://matakia.com.

DAMAGED
RICHARD HOLLEMAN

I missed you today.
I cursed you today.

I can't wait to see you.
I hope I never see
your fucking face again.

Thank you for the damage
you've done. Your careless
hatred has done something
wonderful, almost miraculous.

You gave me the gift
of worthlessness,
to lack self-love.
You stripped meto honest bones.

I cried and clawed
my way to something
different, someone better.
You strengthened me
in ways I couldn't imagine.

No longer do I hide my face
in shame, no longer do I cut
myself for your amusement.
No longer do I yearn for a place
by your side or in your life.

I am right where I belong.

Now I have wrapped a gift
for you. There is no expiration
date, so take your time opening
it if you like. I found it lying
around in my new place;
it is forgiveness,
and it's just for you.

Richard Holleman lives in San Diego, CA where he loves to read and write poetry. Many of his poems directly or indirectly feature a female person he refers to as "Eve." More of his work can be found at https:// richardholleman.weebly.com.

CURTAINS BLOWING IN THE WIND / GOOD BONES
LINDA CASEBEER

CURTAINS BLOWING IN THE WIND

You and I love have written fiction
together it can be an intimate act
where we said writing in and out
of each other elicited the yin yang
of voices the he said she said
but in the year of the unreliable
narrator the question is who
is telling the truth if there is truth
haven't we known all along writers
are unreliable narrators and not all
skeletons are the ones in the closet
like the trendy gone girl
gone missing the story first told
by the adulterous husband
from his point of view also
a suspect but absent a body
did she leave on her own
or is the girlwife framing him
with he said she said is either one
telling the truth if there is a truth
or what about the next story
also a girl witnessing a murder
from the window of a train begging
the question when breath ceases
does the story matter if it is not

murder is there a story to be untold
was the bedroom window
left open that night or locked
who tossed the single white rose
into the river was it a signature
or the return of magic realism
the return of alternate universes

GOOD BONES

Molded of burned lime clay sand gravel
and water mixed into common concrete
a weatherstained slightly cracked angel
gazed up through weeping cherry boughs
overgrown and touching the ground
twenty years after we planted it in honor
of spring or love or something and after we
recorded the garden's history in disappearing
ink when we wanted to trade the steepness
of Red Mountain for what was level
we found ourselves most attached
to the places where we had removed lawn
to make gardens and of it all the realtor
said the house with gardens instead of lawn
would not sell quickly
And yet two months after the sign went up
we sold the house by an English grocer
in 1910 the house built over red boulders
too heavy to move was sold to a single woman
an attorney who had pulled up to the front
curb in her dark blue Mercedes convertible
drawn to the house for its foursquare

brick stature good bones as they say
and the old wood inside once painted
over with flat black before being restored
she loved the house but the deal was not
without the arguments of her profession
she marked up the sales contract
fought over glasses in the kitchen cabinet
along with everything else she could find
Though the angel veiled by cherry boughs
had escaped her notice she also took
possession of it the day of closing
when we left our untidy perennial gardens
originally planted with a design in mind
but grown unto themselves unexpectedly
and we left the angel though the truth is
we had forgotten the barely visible
since the sale we go back to drive past
the house on Red Mountain and find
the angel has been moved into the sun
on the other side of the red brick
walkway amidst the ever intruding
rudbeckia by the new owner who lives
in the four bedroom house alone

Linda Casebeer lives in Birmingham, Alabama and works as a medical education researcher. She has published one collection of poems, The Last Eclipsed Moon, with Cherry Grove Collections, as well as poems in journals such as Pinyon, Earth's Daughters, and Slant.

THE ATHEIST AND THE RAPTURE BUTTON
WILLIAM M. BRANDON III

I

Work is morally compromising. For some, that compromise means retail slavery during the holidays, or slinging drinks for ungrateful inebriated scum. For others, it means protecting something so deeply wrong that we can never be forgiven. My name is Declan by the way, and it's probably a good sign that you are still able to read this.

I'd been searching for more freelance work, but the listings offered only warehouse jobs, wait staff positions, and catering shifts. Though I was desperate enough to take any job I could find, none came within miles of paying my rent. I'd have to take two (sometimes three) of the offered positions to break even. Then, everything changed:

Seeking a Systems Administrator in Hollywood, Ca. Full-time position overseeing complex multi-state customer database and product quality assurance. Must be willing to be on call 24/7. Contact Greg Bahnsen at (469) 282-4464.

I knew my way around a server, but I had no formal training. I felt confident I could tap-dance my way through the interview, start high on salary, and let them back me down. I had to try, it was a quick path to solvency.

I dialed the number in the ad.

"You have reached Greg Bahnsen. Please leave your name, number, and a short message after the tone. Thank you and God bless."

tone

"Hello Mr. Bahnsen. My name Declan Holyoake and I am calling in regard to your advertised position for a Systems Administrator. I have nearly a decade's worth of experience maintaining databases for large and small organizations. I can be reached at (213) 382-5968. I look forward to hearing from you."

I nailed the voicemail.

Jenny, my landlord, called up from her meager backyard.

"Hey, you got a second?"

I descended the spiral staircase from my attic apartment to a narrow strip of landscaped rock and concrete behind Jenny's Hollywood bungalow.

"Hey, are you still looking for work?"

A difficult conversation to have with your landlord. My phone vibrated: *Mom.* I pointed the screen at Jenny and she waved me off, *Mom* could wait.

"I'm always looking for more work."

"We need a doorman on Monday nights at the bar, there's probably two shifts per week that you could pick up."

My phone stopped vibrating. "I have an interview this week that seems really promising." That was a lie. "But I'll stop by regardless." Two lies.

"It's all good; I was just curious." Her lie was the hat trick.

I lit a cigarette to avoid eye contact as Jenny started to walk back into the house. "By the way, have you seen that fucking cat around?"

I kept lying, "Not lately." Jenny had murder on her mind.

"I poured a ton of bleach in the flower bed; if he shits in there again it'll be the last time."

I stared at Jenny the Cat Bleacher with all due horror as I dialed Mom. "Hey, sorry 'bout that. How are you feeling today?"

"I am ok. Every day is a little better." Mom's voice had taken on a plodding, childlike quality after her stroke.

"Your speech is improving."

"Thank you. I try." Mom laughed. "When are you coming to visit?"

The answer was complicated. Rent was on the horizon and I was nowhere near covering it. "As soon as possible Momma."

"I miss you. All I have for company is the internet and old tv shows."

"Rough life eh?"

She couldn't stop laughing. "Ok, I am feeling a little tired, so I will go. I love you."

"I love you too Momma."

"God bless you."

I hung up.

§

Pathos was the only bar in Hollywood without a television, making it a sacred reprieve from the constant din of *my viewpoint* vs. *your viewpoint*. Some nut had ripped the bar's flatscreen from its mooring during the 2016 election, and the locals agreed that change was good. By the time Greg returned my call I'd been at Pathos a few hours and had four pints of stout in me. I hesitated. A non-answer could be a deal breaker, so even though I was getting bleary-eyed, I took the call.

"Good evening. Is this Mr. Bahnsen?"

"Why yes it is, um..."

"Declan."

"Yes, of course. Declan, please call me Greg. Thank you for answering my call. It is very important, as the ad mentioned, that I be able to reach you at critical times day and night."

"I understand."

As I walked out of Pathos, someone whispered over my shoulder: *Perfect. Good move, Declan.* It could have been anyone in the crowded dive.

I leaned against a wall outside. Hollywood Boulevard was busy for a Monday night in January. Back then, Hollywood Boulevard was rarely quiet.

"Declan, I represent a large non-denominational church in Dallas, Texas..."

I was afraid of that...

"...and we are the proud sponsors of *The Greenest Pasture* program. Are you, by any chance, familiar with our work?"

"No sir, I'm not, but I am willing to learn."

"That's just fine. Let me ask you, what do you think of Jesus?"

"Honestly, I try not to if I can help it." It was either vocational suicide or a great ice breaker.

Greg laughed heartily. "Yes, yes, that's perfect, Declan. I feel like you are already a very strong contender for this position. Let's schedule a time for you to come into the office. Are you free this Thursday?"

—it was Tuesday. "Yes sir, I am; all day presently."

"Good, good. Let's say 10 a.m., at 1680 Vine Street, Suite 1212. Does that work?"

"Yes sir, Thank you Mr. Bahn...I mean Greg. I really appreciate this opportunity."

"Don't thank me yet."

I sensed his smile on the other end of the line.

§

I woke, shaved, and showered before 9 a.m. A letter from Mom poked out of the small mailbox on my landlord's porch, so I snatched it for the walk. Between puffs of smoke, I read about Mom's high school classmates getting together for an informal reunion. She expressed surprise and delight that most of them had stayed *god-fearing Americans.*

Mom didn't have much in her life anymore beyond social media. I couldn't tell if loneliness was to blame for her revived spiritual fervor, or if she had reverted to her backward upbringing because it numbed the pain of paralysis. Mom had always been *churchy*, but she seemed to be falling in with the fever of the moment.

Mom mentioned making a big purchase: *with my not-married heathen son in mind.* *sloppy smiley face* *It set us back a little bit, but I want you to know how much I love you.* Her writing became less legible as the letter progressed. I folded it and placed it in my pocket.

An intense little man blocked the doorway of 1680 Vine Street. He wanted to know what my business was, and I thought I detected a military background in his focused, yet pugnacious demeanor. Once I mentioned Greg and he reviewed his clipboard, the man relaxed and showed me to the elevator with a puppy dog's submissive geniality.

The Taft Building was beautiful. The lobby ceiling was vibrantly painted and trimmed, and the floors were greying marble. Decommissioned copper mail chutes lined the walls of the lobby. I examined one and was disappointed that it was bolted shut. I can imagine that people were tempted to put all manner of nonsense into those chutes in the age of email, but it was still a shame. The rickety elevator rolled slowly to the twelfth floor and I made a mental note to take the stairs when possible.

The door to suite 1212 lay at the south end of the long hallway and had chipped, recently re-applied, white paint covering it from frame to hinge to threshold. I knocked carefully but confidently on the door and a man answered.

"Come in, Declan, I'm Greg." Greg was one of those poor chaps who ages faster than nature intended. Though his baby face said *late twenties*, his jowls and receding hairline screamed *just shy of sixty*.

"I'll give you the grand tour. This will be your station," Greg pointed to a large desk equipped with a modern desktop PC and several file organizers. "Here is the server room," Greg pointed to a room buzzing with equipment and air conditioning systems. "And I'm in the back near the fire escape."

Greg's office was barren save for a another large desk, a similar desktop PC, and no signs of actual work.

"I'm only here to make sure the Systems Admin. is comfortable and competent. Then, I make my way back to Texas." Greg gestured to a small round table in the corner of his office. "Please have a seat." He folded his hands over a stack of documents. "I only have a few routine questions for you. First, are you a member of any local worship centers or worship organizations?"

"No sir." I figured honesty was still the best policy, although pretending to be a bible-thumper did cross my mind.

"Excellent. Any church activities at all?"

"No sir."

"Out of laziness, or..." He let the question hang.

"I'm what you might call a practicing atheist, Greg."

Greg's eyes lit up. "Perfect! Do you have any problems with signing a non-disclosure agreement?"

"None whatsoever."

"Splendid. Let's get that out of the way before we proceed. I think you are our man, Declan." Greg smiled: just shy of a used car salesman and slightly more devious than your run-of-the-mill proselytizer.

"I need to ask one further question. Are you willing to be on-call twenty-four hours per day and seven days per week?"

"Yes."

"We require that you move into this facility. The office suite down the hall has been equipped with requisite sleeping and cooking arrangements; consider it a perk of the job. You will receive full health benefits, and a salary of one hundred thousand dollars before taxes."

My jaw dropped.

"You will be responsible for maintaining this office and all of its paperwork while I am away, but your primary responsibility will be to make sure they," Greg pointed to the server room, "keep running day and night. You will remain onsite from 8 a.m. until 5 p.m. in case we have any unexpected visitors, or if I need your assistance in some way. The keypad for the server room requires a retinal scan. Any questions so far?"

"Yes, what are the servers running?"

"They maintain the database and operational data for *The Greenest Pasture*."

"The suspense is killing me," I joked.

"As a formality, I'd like to officially offer you the position before we discuss the program's details."

"Thank you Greg! I accept wholeheartedly."

"Wonderful, then it's official, welcome to the family. I can be forthcoming now; part of the reason I chose you is that you are an atheist."

"I was getting that impression. Churches don't usually hire dirty heathens do they?"

"This job is a bit different. Years ago, our founder recognized that there were millions of believers who were born and raised in the church that would be left behind by the Rapture: husbands and wives, sons and daughters, Mayors and Presidents. Do you know what the Rapture is?"

"Yes, my Mom is a dyed-in-the-wool Southern Baptist."

"Once the Rapture is complete, the persons left behind will have another opportunity to repent, and that's where we come in. *The Greenest Pasture* delivers a digital message from the Saved to their damned loved ones. Our subscribers know that someone they love will reject the gift of Christ's blood—until it is too late."

I grew up with all of the religious code words and scare tactics, but I cringed anyway.

"I can see that you are truly devoid of faith, Declan. Only a person of your profound ignorance—no offense," Greg smiled, "can be trusted to remain on Earth and send these messages from our Raptured congregation."

"I get it; I'm the atheist waiting to press the Rapture button."

"Something like that. In the end, God's will is being done, even by an atheist. Isn't God amazing?"

"Did the last guy..."

"Yes. Stephen Patrick accepted Christ as his Lord and Savior last month, God bless him. He lost his job but gained eternity at the right hand of Christ."

"My good fortune it seems."

"Stephen Patrick's conversion reminded us that the great state of Texas is God's country. The board decided to move the operation to one of the few remaining regions dense with non-believers. I was tasked with finding a Systems Administrator who would be guaranteed to push the button. Can we count on you, Declan?"

"I am a devout non-believer, and neither you, nor an army of snake-handling televangelists will ever change that." I intended to remain a dirty heathen, collect my tidy salary, and wait for an apocalypse that was never coming.

"Declan," Greg rose to shake my hand, "welcome to *The Greenest Pasture*."

II

Jenny the Cat Bleacher was surprised. It felt good to tell her I was leaving. She asked about my new job because she thought she should, but I told her not to worry about it. I planned on paying for the rest of the month in a couple of days.

She smiled, "Oh, well thank you. It'll be weird for the attic to be empty again."

I started to climb the spiral staircase and didn't respond.

I moved my box and a half of belongings into suite 1204 early the following Sunday morning. The doorman let me into the suite, and as soon I had set my box down, my phone buzzed.

"Declan, it's Greg."

"I figured. I'm getting myself moved in."

"So I see. Don't worry, your room is devoid of monitoring devices but the rest of the building is...well, no one will be stealing our doughnuts, eh?"

"Shouldn't you be at church Greg?"

"I'm dropping by the office for a moment before I go."

Greg stepped from the elevator in his Sunday best.

"Wow boss, looking sharp."

"Thank you Declan. So, are you settled in?"

"I am."

"Excellent. Stephen Patrick was a meticulous record keeper, and he canonized all procedures and processes prior to leaving. In his words you should be able to pick right up and run.

"Here are the physical keys to the shop and your passcard. Both the key and the passcard are necessary to lock the doors. If you lose these items, contact me immediately and maintain visual surveillance over the office."

"No problem Greg. Are you turning me loose?"

"Yes, your confidence is contagious. I booked a flight for shortly after this morning's service at Bel Air Presbyterian. There is a very special young lady I want a chance to speak to before I return to Texas."

"Greg, you sly dog, you."

Greg smiled, "Well, we'll see won't we?"

§

I ended up in Pathos, but I waited until 5pm in case Greg was still watching. As I opened the door, bright daylight penetrated the tomb-like bar. The unwelcome sunshine served as a reminder that the world carried on just beyond the afternoon stupor.

I ordered a stout, and the bartender snapped his fingers, remembering something important. "Watch out for the guys on the corner. They're not real cops; they're worse. Anyway, my shift is over." I handed him a five dollar bill. "Thanks, be careful out there."

I shared the bar with one other patron. He had his head bowed toward a half-empty yellow beer. His gaunt cheeks, bony hands, and disheveled hair, painted a portrait of dedicated self-destruction.

I heard the voice whisper over my shoulder again.

Goddamn church is getting obnoxious, Declan.

"How do you know my name?"

I don't know your name, Declan.

My barmate never lifted his head.

"Great, a ventriloquist and an asshole."

The bartender was talking about the men on the corner. They belong to the Civility Guard.

I ignored him. The new bartender said hello, but seemed not to notice the corpse whispering to me.

Being 'mad with drink' is a punishable offense.

"Look pal, as far as I can tell we're strangers. Let's keep it that way."

You hate pushy people. I am not a pushy person by nature, but you are being more stubborn than I had anticipated.

"I don't know what any of that means, but I'm here to celebrate being employed." I motioned to the new bartender, "A stout for myself, and another of whatever this gentleman likes." I turned back to the stranger. "Now, I've offered a gesture of goodwill. Please leave me be."

The new bartender sighed wearily. "It's just you and me cowboy, and I'm in the Program. You want that second drink now, or later?"

The strange man was still hunched over his yellow beer. How did the bartender not see him? I felt nauseated.

Don't throw up. This is the only place I can speak freely with you.

"I didn't ask for this. Whatever is happening is not okay with me..."

The man raised his forlorn eyes and nodded. I blinked, and he was gone.

I downed the stout and waved to the bartender, "Make the second a whiskey neat. Whatever you have that doesn't come from a plastic bottle."

Monday morning hurt. I drank long into the night trying to conjure the man, but he never returned. I felt like a bundle of mistakes, and the dehydration only gave my regret a physical dimension.

Not the best way to start a job, but I've failed harder without trying. I had hot coffee on my desk and all systems running through process logging in twenty minutes.

Greg texted—*Back in God's country, amen. Thank you for being punctual. I trust you have everything you need, if not let me know. May God bless us all.*

I replied—*Glad you are home safe, and will do.*

—*Did you see that speech in Iowa last night? Man, I've never been this excited about a President. He really is of the People.*

—*Didn't see it.*

—*Good thing, our President has the power of persuasion.*

If you're a brain dead moron, sure...

I had a lot of reading to do.

§

After a few paychecks, I could finally afford to have lunch in the neighborhood, something other than tacos or a cheap sandwich—3/4 bread 1/4 meatcheesewhatever. I grabbed a short booth in the last hipster diner on Ivar Street. All of the businesses that came to the neighborhood via gentrification, were long gone. When it became clear that the impoverished and criminal were not leaving Hollywood without a fight, investors got spooked and sent their development money Downtown, where it's 3 cops to each citizen.

Every television was tuned to the President's favorite news outlet. It's hard to block it out, but you have to try. There aren't many true believers in Hollywood, which is why I stuck around, but local businesses kept the sainted news channel on twenty-four hours per day, like a great shrieking mouth.

Greg texted—*Happy month-a-versary!*

—*Thanks! All is well.*

—*I know. How is your spiritual struggle?*

—*Non existent.*

—*Amen.*

The only waitress in the diner stood behind the bar with the only bartender and the host. They were staring blankly at the President, whose twisted face consumed the HD monitor hung above the horseshoe-shaped bar. Someone turned the volume up.

Folks...folks, look, a problem, yes. We have many of them, things that aren't right. So true...but now, people are speaking, with tongues, and lips, and voices. A wonderful thing to see, to taste, and hear. Because of this I cannot stand by, yes I have tears here folks, believe me. I cannot allow good god-fearing people to be abused. Across our waving nation of greatness...Yes, sea to ocean, to desert, patriots communing with groups of like-minded Americans, patriots like our own George Washington for instance. Fighting, and fighting what is right, always. So, of course, we are federally funding these groups. What are they?" *offcamera whispering* "Yes, City Guard Posts. Guards, folks, Civility Guards I'm told. They're here to make you live a better life. Are they cops? Maybe, who cares? They care. About crime. And terrorists. About people determined to destroy the undestroyable love of Christ Jesus. Can't be destroyed folks. Even Allah knows. These guards, crusaders really, will clean up our streets, keep an eye on those who bring harm, and mess with our way of life. Can't tread on us Liberals. No means no.

Am I right? Folks... In the end, through me, mostly through me, God's will is being done.

The bartender, "Does anyone know what that idiot is rambling about?"

The waitress, "He's drunk. He has to be."

The host, "He's talking about church police. Like, walking around calling people out for cussing and short skirts."

The waitress, "You have to be kidding."

The host, "They've been around for a long time. They used to protest at funerals for famous homosexuals and atheists. They think they are doing god's work. Most people ignore them, obviously they are whacked. But now, I mean look who our President is..."

The bartender, "Yeah, well, watch yourself. Saying shit like that will get you fired."

The host, "Fuck 'em. Silence is guilt."

The waitress, "Complicity. Silence is complicity."

The host, "Oh, guys, there's someone here."

The waitress walked toward me craning her neck to see the screen.

"Hey."

"Hello." I smiled but for naught. "Bacon and eggs, lots of coffee, and a double whiskey neat. Irish whiskey if you have it."

"Cool. Did you come here for the Emergency Text Party? It got cancelled, you know."

"No. Just here for lunch. What's the Emergency Text party?"

The waitress pointed to a poster in the doorway. "Protest of some sort. Against the President's emergency warning thing-a-ma-bob. Rumor has it someone squealed and the whole party had to go underground."

"I guess I'm a little behind on the times."

She walked toward the kitchen watching the screen intently.

Jenny the Cat Bleacher was waiting at the entrance to the Taft building when I returned.

"Finally." Her hand was frantically tapping out a cigarette. "You forgot to leave your new number and address. I remembered you said something about working here, so, yeah. I have mail for you." She reached into her handbag and produced several envelopes.

"Thanks, I appreciate that. I have the same number, I can't imagine why I didn't see your calls..." I opened the lobby door.

"Aren't you going to show me your new office?"

I smiled and closed the door behind me.

Mom's penmanship was improving, but more and more, she was speaking in someone else's voice. *My son, I know you don't get involved in politics, but there are dangerous people flooding into this country, taking good jobs from Americans like Robert, and trying to destroy our way of life. Our President is taking care of them. He is restoring our pride.* The fear of foreign invasion came from her news stories, perhaps my stepfather. *Sometimes you just have to go back to your heritage. You have to stand up for what the country means. I am sad about what is happening, but the President gives me hope.* Mom continued to hint at the big surprise I had in store; I couldn't decide if she was building tension or forgetting she had mentioned it. What was clear: she was gleefully preparing for war, and for someone in her condition, that was an unhealthy focus.

I walked to a nearby liquor store, and took home a bottle of Irish brown—breaking my cardinal rule: never drink at home, especially alone. The possibility of a conversation with the whispering man was good enough to keep me away from Pathos, and everywhere else had that abominable news station blaring.

As the elevator crept to a stop on the twelfth floor, my phone buzzed.

PRESIDENTIAL ALERT

THIS IS A TEST of the President's Communication Network. All is well, this is only a test. God bless our United State.

Everyone was looking at their phone. Some were bewildered—I could relate—some smirked, and some shook their heads in resignation. I pulled up my own news stories and was disappointed to find our President had sent every last American a text message, whether they liked it or not. They did not provide an opportunity to opt-out.

It was an absurd violation: soft but penetrating. Privacy is only a marketing term; it was simple to look the other way and blame our vulnerability on our need to connect. The reality was much darker, much harder to swallow.

—*Did you get it?* Another text, Mom this time.

—*Yeah. Pretty creepy.*

—**look of confusion emoticon**

—*The Presidential text message, it's creepy*

—*No. My letter*

—*Yes. I'll write back tonight*

—*You are a good son*

III

I decided to explain to Mom the millions of reasons she was wrong in long form rather than text message—wrong about politics, wrong about America, and wrong about our outlandish President. Maybe a little subtle chipping at the more ridiculous aspects of her newfound cult would bring her around. Mom had always been an *obey first, ask questions later* sort of American, but this felt like something different.

The letter I wrote asked if she'd considered the hardships of the people she demonized. I didn't go any further, I imagined her tearfully reading my response, forever stuck in that bed, and I became weak. I went on to talk about my new job and it's intriguing secrecy. I knew she'd be impressed that her son was finally doing something productive—religiously positive—and to my discredit, I was desperate for any way to make her days less bleak.

I dropped the letter into the only post box I could find and headed up to the office. Greg called as soon as I crossed the threshold.

"Greg man, that's kind of creepy."

"We have a problem. This is not a phone conversation."

"Ok, I know how to reach you."

I spun up a VPN and began an encrypted conversation with Greg.

—*A security breach was just detected. Per our team, a lethal injection attack placed executable code into the database. The next person that purchases a subscription will trigger a worm and replicate it throughout all connected devices.*

Greg was relying on the information provided to him, otherwise he'd know it's called a *SQL* injection attack. —*Sounds like they got in through the app, I know what to do on my end.*

I set to work determining whether my system had been compromised. Everything was coming up clean and passing inspection. Three small clusters of commands flashed by in the log for database credentialing. I scrolled back and found what I was looking for.

—*The system was not compromised, Greg. I'm happy to report that the foreign code was isolated, triggered reporting in the appropriate logs, and never engaged with the server processes or had an opportunity to replicate.*

—*That is a relief. Good job Declan. Send your report through this encryption key and then wipe it from your hard drive.*

—*It's only really clean when it's been burned to ash.*

—*That won't be necessary Declan, you passed the test.*

They were already testing me.

§

The strange man was sitting at the end of the bar in the dark. I decided to take the seat next to him. His hands looked fragile: spindly and wrapped 'round his pint glass, still not quite empty. Pathos had hired another bartender. Their turnover made gaining *local* status impossible.

I motioned to the current bartender and waited as she helped everyone else. I could feel my shadow waiting to speak. "What do you want from me?"

Want. That's very interesting, I haven't considered our situation from that perspective.

"Our situation is the prelude to a restraining order..."

You're not convinced I'm real, Declan. Let's not be coy.

"Fine. At least tell me your name..."

The man turned his head and did not answer. He had wasted away since our last encounter. His face was gaunt, hollow, and his skin had greyed to the pallor of necrotic disease. Before thinking, I asked, "Are you ill?"

Sickness pervades and penetrates our every waking moment Declan. You can feel the rampant, naked aggression as it foments ancient rifts. Those that cling to the past, stand headlong against the world to come.

"Everything seems to be changing. I'll give you that, but I've been alive too long to fall for the *this is the end* spiel."

Of course, and to what end should we concern ourselves with the end, anyway? There will be more bloodshed Declan, of that, we can all be assured. The time to dam the floods has passed, now is the time to choose a shore.

"Jersey Shore."

That was funny.

My phone buzzed, but it didn't matter. "What are you afraid is coming?" The thin man was gone. I checked my phone, *Mom* again. I dialed as I walked out onto Hollywood Boulevard.

"What's up old lady?"

"Old lady? If I weren't in a wheelchair..."

Mom laughed. It always felt a little better when she laughed.

"So how's the weather in Vegas?"

"Hot, very hot. But we have good AC. God has truly blessed us."

"No, Robert's military benefits have truly blessed you."

"True, but the Lord God is working harder every day, you can see it happening."

"Right, in the rosy cheeks of a child, and the morning dew on a velvety clover..."

"No," she laughed, "it's even better. Abortion will be illegal soon."

Her glee disturbed me. "Not without overturning federal law..."

"You should watch the news." Her speech came slowly. "The Supreme Court voted."

"Wait, Mom, that's not a good thing. Roe vs. Wade isn't about a medical procedure."

"But killing babies is a sin, and we've angered God enough. Our President finally put someone on the court that understands that."

"I thought that guy turned out to be some sort of frat boy date-rapist."

"No, that was a conspiracy by the Left, trying to destroy a good god-fearing conservative man."

It was my turn to laugh. "I didn't pay much attention, but I can guarantee that if your President nominated him, he's neither good nor god-fearing."

"It is part of a plan by the Left to..."

"Mom, do you know what *The Left* is?"

"Communists."

"Well, partly. Democrats are *The Left* too."

"They are worse than communists, they are American communists." Mom wasn't really able to raise her voice anymore, but she would have, right then.

"Democrats are definitely worse than communists, but for the same reasons Republicans are worse than communists."

"I don't like any of them. They're all crooked." —it was the most forward-thinking thing I had heard her say in years— "But I thank God and the Republican party for giving us our President. He will make sure that in the end, God's will is done."

"What did you say?"

"I don't like any of them. They all lie ..."

"No, just now, it felt familiar."

"Hold on son."—My stepfather asked Mom about taking his fishing boat out for the weekend—"Sorry, Robert needed to ask me something."

"I heard. Fishin' eh? Are you going along?"

"No, the chair is too heavy for the boat. Besides, why would I want to go fishing?" She laughed again.

"Touché, but you'll be alone for a long time."

"Oh it's ok, I'm used to it," more laughter, but to my ears bitter. "Robert takes very good care of me. He even took extra shifts the past two weeks."

"Are you guys cool?"

"Well, we're having a little trouble this month."

"How much do you need?"

"Nine hundred."

"Don't worry about it, I'll transfer the money as soon as we get off the phone." It felt strange to be able to conjure up that kind of money.

"Thank you son, Robert and I appreciate it."

"It's no problem. How did you guys get messed up for nine hundred bucks?"

"Oh, it was just a mistake. I have a subscription and there was an error. They charged my account twice."

"Are they going to fix it?"

"Yes. I have already called them. Our next month will be free." Mom giggled, proud of the accommodation.

"Well, it's not really free since you have already paid for it. And to make you wait instead of refunding the money, sounds shady to me."

"It's ok, I have a successful son who can help me."

"If you didn't, you'd be in trouble."

"That's true. I love you."

"I love you too Momma. I need to jump off the phone..."

"Ok, thanks for calling me back. God bless..."

You are a good son.
The whispering man returned.
We sat in silence until Pathos closed its doors.

§

Sleep was impossible. I wandered the office, fixed coffee, and smoked on the fire escape as the sun rose over south Vine Street. I tried to imagine the coming day as a reminder of Mom's benevolent god, as if the nourishment of the planet was ultimately *god's will*.

That was what I had heard, *god's will*. Mom said it, Greg said it, and above all, their Dear Leader said it. I rushed to my computer and scanned the offending code from the prior night's *test*. Hackers are humans and they can't fight their natural tendency toward failure. To find that failure, you just have to be able to see everything at once.

The attacker knew all about my system, so I decided to start with the entry point. I needed to see what, if anything, looked like untoward processes. I was able to isolate seven functions that failed to execute. Buried within a long string, I found the seven-digit serial number for the seventh encryption code on the list from Greg.

The attack was recycled: either copied from a better coder, or previously deployed, but the work was sloppy: my overseer had forgotten to remove his bridge back into the main system. Since he never really left the home network, the escape door lay dormant and unused.

Being underestimated by my employer's spies gave me the advantage, and the developing web of ominous intentions made it impossible for me to stay out. I wouldn't last long once I got inside, but if I could sneak a peek of what they were hiding, I'd get a better picture of *who* I was working for.

My guess about the encryption code proved correct. I was in with no hassle, and as far as I could tell, I wasn't setting off any alarms, so to speak. As I combed through directory listings I couldn't shake the feeling that all of this was a little too easy. Sure, I had a key to the door, but the only person authorized to use that key was verifiably in Texas. It was like something more important was sucking up all the attention.

The directories were a series of individual databases, each containing descriptions in a company lexicon, and what appeared to be digital coordinates for groups of data. *The Greenest Pasture* only existed on my side of the fence, which meant that we were feeding data into whatever was behind these databases. Encryption codes six and three, used in combination, opened the pathway from my little World into the larger Universe.

She was in there, my Mom. I was in there as well, listed as *the damned*. The gift she had beamed about was her raptured message to me:

My poor lost son, I am sad about what is happening,
but I am at peace because I know that in the end,
God's will is being done.

I wasn't shocked, but my eyes filled with tears regardless.

IV

I kept to chain restaurants, bustling plazas, and busy coffee shops—anywhere with a tv—until the tingling ends of my nerves numbed.

The din of narcotized Presidential pronouncements faded far left of field and I sat there, day after day tending to my legion of parked condescending missives.

I tried hard to think of the money I was making instead of the vile undercurrent of hypocrisy I was shoring up. The subscriptions ranged from one hundred dollars per month for a standard *Wish you were here*, to the deluxe $1000 soul-crushing guilt subscription which laid out in great personal detail, every last thing your Raptured loved one thought you had done to deserve eternal hellfire.

I tried hard to think about the hope, deluded as it is, that belief gives to those hungry to judge. Most people had their minds tampered with at a young age, and it's hard for anyone to walk back that foundation. I can testify.

We are receiving new reports that an Associate Justice of the Supreme Court is in critical condition at an undisclosed location. It appears to have been a failed assassination. The DC Metro Police have no suspects, and at this time claim they have no leads. The Justice's spokesperson just gave a press statement over the phone.

...She was attacked in broad daylight, by persons who were intimately aware of her movements. Just like all of her peers before her. We cannot pretend that these systematic murders are a coincidence. We cannot remain silent when the media won't even say her name...

We all wish the Associate Justice a very speedy recovery. With only one Justice remaining, the President could very well remake the entire court in his image within the year. We live in very exciting times, right Sarah?

"Wait," the news story cut through, "when did that happen? They replaced eight Supreme Court Judges?"

"You got me buddy, who cares? Bunch of criminals anyway. You need a refill or what?" The bartender assumed, correctly, that I had just pulled out of a drunken haze.

"No, I'm good. I'm being serious, that's never happened before. Not in this country."

"What the hell do you know? No one gives a shit what you think unless you are a job-provider. We finally have a government that understands us."

"I feel like I know more, it's just all jumbled..."

"Here's the thing, if you don't like it, you can move to another country, problem solved."

I couldn't believe people still said things like that. I tipped poorly and left.

As I stumbled down Selma Avenue my phone buzzed again. I was in no shape to talk to anyone, it would have to wait. I made it to Pathos right before the evening crowd intensified, and pulled up a stool near the end of the bar. I ordered a glass of water and sat in the dark, refusing to drink until the sick man appeared.

You are already drunk Declan, what are you trying to prove?

"That I still have some control."

The man whispered but would not appear. *Control. That's a very loaded word. You should check your text messages.*

"No thanks. Probably..."

It's not your mom.

"Ah, there you are." I looked the dying man in the eye, and his flesh hung tenuously from his skull. When I turned to ignore him, his cast reflection behind the bar was skeletal.

You should check your text messages.

8pm
PRESIDENTIAL ALERT
We call upon our people to express their Faith through prayer. This concludes your day of Worship. God bless our United State.

The alert comes three times a day, if you're into that sort of thing.

"For the record, I'm not."

61

Doesn't matter, does it? You get the message from El Presidente just like the rest of the morons.

"I'm pretty sure someone will tie this up in court. You can't just..."

Which court Declan? There aren't any left.

"They can send me messages about gods and godlike things until they are blue in the face. You're right, it *doesn't* matter."

Here's a thought. Maybe you're right, and there is no god. Maybe there's only an agreement to keep that a secret. Secrets have always had supernatural power.

"The Congress hasn't presented legislation in years, they just provide legal cover for the President's Executive Orders." I wasn't sure how I knew that, or why I said it.

Look around Declan, this is our world now. It's not coming, it's been here for a long time. Your apathy never protected you.

"My apathy? I'm not responsible for this..."

But you are Declan, responsible for every encroaching inch, each creeping schism you ignored because it did not affect your life. None of that matters now. What else did you see while you were inside the system, Declan?

"My mom..."

...Is a racist little troll. What else Declan? What were you trying to forget?

Her ugliness had been enough, and the realization that as I apologized for her cruel beliefs, I had only stacked brick and mortar against her Wall.

"It's an incredible eye."

Yes.

"They are watching at all times."

Yes.

"Labeling us unCivil when we think."

Yes. Your little pity party about dear old Mom is complicity.

"I can't bear to lose her, or this job, or my station in this new society."

Why do you think they hired you? Greg knows you're weak, he knows your weaknesses. You were cheap to dazzle, and cheap to maintain. A little funny business with dear old Mom's records brought you to heel, reminded you of your responsibilities, *without lifting a finger.*

The dying man's flesh had fallen completely away. To his audience of one, he presented only his raw core, nothing but hollow clacking bones devoid of sinew, devoid of mass.

"Then it doesn't matter what I do."

It never has.

"I should look after myself."

Yes.

§

The vast universe beyond the flagging databases was a churning cauldron. Data sets grew and evaporated like bricks in a massive breathing barrier. By freeing the data from structure, the system could devour information with reckless abandon and maximize storage potential. No thought was given to what *is*, or *is not*, important. The great eye's mission was only to collect and accuse.

I wrote a short, three-part script and introduced it into the main system via USB thumb drive. I waved to the cameras in the server room before locking the doors to the suite. The elegant—if I do say so myself—lines of code corrupted the flagging databases and rendered the massive stockpile of personal data a seething, chaotic mass, impossible to detangle. Before self-destructing, so to speak, the attack sent the paid-for messages of condemnation to *the damned*, en masse.

§

My actions were redemptive kindling
amidst a firestorm.

I should have gone farther,
but it was the last chance I got.

William began his lifelong roadtrip in the deprecated sands of Las Vegas, Nevada. As a result of a military patriarch, and unabated restlessness, has changed addresses fifty-six times in forty-two years. He is a father, a husband, and his work has been published by The Rumpus, in a special anthology supporting Mines Advisory Group, in the not-for-profit fiction anthology The Cost of Paper, and novella SILENCE was published by Black Hill Press.

SKELETONS
NANCY HOOPER

Unaware of the wind or the weight
of the dust that will bury.
There will be no farewell
when the earth closes in. No fear
of the darkness surrounding.
The rain rains and the mud sucks.
Leaves skitter and catch in our ribs,
but we can not assume that much,
or feel to quiver underneath the touch.
What injustice? What inhumanity?
We do not ask, or long for our recovery,
or know that we were lost.
There are no remnants of these things.
Just a puzzle of bones,
and this song the wind whistles between.
But even this we do not know,
or anticipate the crumble beneath the crush,
or wonder that we smile so much.

Nancy Hooper lives and works in Ypsilanti, Michigan with her husband, Tim, and their cat, Avalanche. Her poetry has appeared in The MacGuffin literary journal, including her chapbook, "Thunder and Other Things".

MARROW

M. HOWALT

This is the story of two overgrown boys on a road trip. You have probably heard it before, but I personally feel that the focus is always slightly off when others tell it. So let me do the talking for once, okay?

It was all Loki's fault, of course. It pretty much always is. I'd be surprised if he didn't suggest the road trip in the first place. He probably did the packing too which would explain why they brought along an arsenal of weapons, spare shoes, fresh underwear, extra cloaks for cold weather and lots of mead and completely neglected to bring food and water or a tent. But fine. I suppose there was marginally less for us to haul along like that, and my brother and I just need a patch of grass to nibble on.

We dragged the carriage all the way across Bifrost, from Asgard to Midgard, and onto bumpy roads with gravel that got stuck between our toes more than once. Back then, Thor and Loki were caught up in their bromance, boasting to each other, making ridiculous bets, drinking and singing while my brother and I could do nothing but roll our eyes and send each other meaningful looks.

When night approached on the first day of the Midgard leg of the road trip, Thor blamed Loki for not bringing a tent, and Loki blamed Thor for not reminding him to bring a tent, and so on. Luckily there was a farmhouse nearby where they decided to stay. Yes, that's how the gods roll. Normal people would have found an inn somewhere or at least approached the people they were about to intrude on with a bit of humility, but not those guys. Thor just knocked on the door and told the woman who opened it that he and his friend needed some supper and a place to stay overnight.

She wasn't stupid. She knew a god when she saw one. From where I was standing, I could clearly make out the complicated emotions on the poor woman's face. Awe that she was in the presence of Thor. Worry that her humble abode might not please him. And something else. She only had a few vegetables in her pantry, she explained. Nothing that would quell the hunger of weary travelers, and even less so when they were infamous of imbibing huge quantities of food. The last bit she didn't say.

"That's no problem," Thor said and made a gesture with his thumb over his shoulder.

Well, shit. My brother and I knew where that was going. We'd been through it before. And let me tell you right away, it sucks like nobody's business every single time.

The woman shot us a glance, and I bleated a request to just serve the bloody vegetables, but she didn't get it. Instead she showed Thor into the farmhouse where, I expect, he became acquainted with the whole family.

Meanwhile, Loki unpacked and unharnessed us. He didn't fail to pinch our buttocks and smack his lips and wiggle his eyebrows at us. I mean, seriously? When the only redeeming feature a friendly billy goat can think of about a person is their lack of sexual interest, apart from that one time when said person transformed into a pretty lady goat, which is a story none of us like to talk about, thank you very much, then there is something seriously wrong with that person.

Anyway, the beanstalk son of the farmer came out of the house, and Loki told him to help out, which he did. Some of the trickster's infamous witty bantering and kicking-the-wheels of the carriage ensued.

"Can we really eat them?" the boy asked, which isn't particularly polite right in front of the meal-to-be, but kudos for critical thinking anyway.

"Sure," Loki replied brightly. "You haven't tasted tender meat till you've tasted these." Another pinch, this time right in the part of my midsection that I'm actually a bit self-conscious about. "Even the worst cook can make a meal fit for kings if they use those two. But ..." He coughed into his hand and stole a glance around to see if Thor was nearby. "If you want the best part, you have to try the marrow."

The boy nodded, infatuated with Loki like everyone else who didn't know him. "I will," he said.

"Only," Loki added, making a brisk sidestep as I swung around to land my back hooves in his grinning face, "Thor is a real hard-ass when it comes to these things. He wants all the marrow for himself, so you have to be a bit ... shall we say discreet?"

"Oh," the boy said and bit his lip.

I tried to catch his attention with an indignant bleat, and my brother lowered his horns and began to close in on Loki.

"Here you go," Loki continued, fishing a small knife out of his pocket. "This is sharp enough to cut through bone with no problem. It's a gift. Unless," and here his voice took on a jeering quality, "you are too scared? Thor is big and dumb. He won't know. I dare you to do it. Call it ... a test of your manhood."

Can we just take a moment to talk about toxic masculinity here? I mean, come on! But the boy took the knife, and Loki had to retreat from our horns and hooves very quickly. He had hardly left before Thor appeared with his big hunting knife.

This is one of the parts other narrators of this tale choose to skip over really fast. And sure, it is pretty quick when he does it, but it is still a very upsetting and very painful and somewhat traumatizing experience. Imagine dying. Time and time again. Then add the agony and the feeling that the guy you work for shouldn't brutally slaughter you just because he can. Having one's throat slit is one of those things that is not supposed to happen, and if it does, it's supposed to be the last thing you feel. Ever.

After the deed was done, I have no recollection of what happened for the remainder of the night. But I can make a qualified guess.

We were skinned. We were chopped into little pieces. We were boiled with root vegetables and seasoned with salt and herbs. We were ladled into bowls and shoveled into mouths. We were chewed into a pulp, swallowed, and washed down with mead. And complimented for our great taste, I'm sure.

The next morning, Thor took our hides and our bones outside with him to magically reconstruct us by swinging his hammer Mjolnir over our remains while our meat was still working its way through his digestive system. Don't ask me how that works, by the way. With gods, there sometimes is no logical linear consequence. Thor can indeed be full of the meat of the goats that are pulling his carriage while he is still belching from the meal. Just go with it. It's not worth it to be driven mad by the paradox.

Anyway, there I was again, magically whole and standing next to my brother who looked every bit as miffed about the whole thing as I felt. Only, I felt something else too. Something completely wrong with my left hind leg. It hurt, and I could barely stand on it.

Thor was grinning and congratulating himself on a job well done when I limped over to him with an accusatory stare. The grin disappeared. The thunder god turned around and roared, bringing out the woman and the boy and the farmer and a small girl too, presumably the whole family, with his tantrum. Now, it wasn't exactly animal rights he was going on about here. It was mostly about how someone had screwed up his property and gone against his rules and how he would have to walk now that one of the goats clearly couldn't work for him with a broken leg. Let's appreciate the irony in that. But okay, we can walk across the sky in a way that most of the aesir can't.

Loki, naturally, was nowhere to be seen. Eventually, the boy admitted that he had sliced open one of my bones and sucked out the marrow. No one told him to apologie to the victim of his crime, but at least he had the decency to avoid my glare and sob a bit.

69

The mess was settled by an arrangement that my brother and I should stay with the farmer and his family to allow me to recuperate while Thor and Loki brought along the boy to carry their luggage on the road trip-turned-hike. Then they would come back for us on the way home and also take the girl along as a servant. This was supposedly an honor to the family, although some people may consider it child labour.

All thing considered, however, the well-deserved holiday that my brother and I got with a family who tended to our every needs and treated us as gods was almost worth that broken bone. Let's not call that the moral of the story, though. I'm just telling you all this for awareness reasons, you know?

Physically located in the Nordic kingdom Denmark, Marie Howalt explores other dimensions by writing character-driven fiction taking place in the far future, fantasy worlds and alternate realities. Marie's post-apocalyptic debut novel, We Lost the Sky, was published by Spaceboy Books in 2019, and its sequel will be released in 2020.

Marie grew up with stories from Norse mythology, but although they weren't the reason behind becoming a vegetarian, they probably were what caused Marie to always feel really iffy about bone marrow.

Say hi on Twitter or Instagram @mhowalt, drop by http://www.mhowalt.dk, or check out http://www.patreon.com/mariehowalt for more speculative fiction.

POST-DIGITAL BUDDHAHOOD
SUDEEP ADHIKARI

a single millisecond of pure
watchfulness, and all the hell starts
to break loose. a psychic
quake shakes your polymer-sheaths
revealing the voids beneath
your bones and dust. a pure
violence consumes you

and everything goes disconnected
like the cantor's dust. no matter how deep
you zoom in, there are these
pockets of unknown mysteriously fitting
between your every self-affirmed
reality-checks; the same way
those cold galactic voids,
tessellate our telescopic comfort-zones
of pulsars and colored Jupiters.

but you can't take a selfie
of your soul, and see where you
need to filter your scars. so i make

home for my boolean digits, between
me and my thousand buddhahoods.

unborn, yet with thousand faces.
deathless, yet murdered each moment.

Sudeep Adhikari is a structural engineer/Lecturer from Kathmandu, Nepal. His recent publications were with Beatnik Cowboys, Chiron Review, The Ekphrastic Review, Midnight Lane Boutique, Occulum, Silver Birch Press, Eunoia Review, Utt Poetry and Spilling Cocoa over Martin Amis. Also a Pushcart Prize nominee for the year 2018, Sudeep is currently working on his 4th poetry-book "Hyper-Real Reboots", which is scheduled for publication in September 2018 through Weasel Press, Texas, USA.

LINGULATE
MEGAN DENESE MEALOR

Tigerish thunderheads
slouch on the skylight,
rime fumes overarching
forced forsythia.

Your undiluted staccato
is a snarling abattoir,
padlocked and piqued,
a red-letter pentameter.

Your acrobatic composition
swaggers like a skinhead's
bluebeat bomber,
a pliant chorine's
hothouse bones.

Within a maelstrom of
astrobleme acoustics
and Lila Kedrova
background batter,
we unbolt birdcages,
unlatch orchestrinas,
unlace lamplit shackles.

I am handleless, halcyon
until the emphasis
of your inception,

the lilac momentum
of your stem.

Beyond this backstage brickwork,
pavement pachinko dwells,
bandaged and balletic,
bobsy-die chanticleers
cantillating chalkdowns.

Megan Denese Mealor is a double Pushcart Prize nominee. Her work has been featured in numerous journals, including The Opiate, Maudlin House, The Metaworker, The Ministry of Poetic Affairs, and Harbinger Asylum. Her debut poetry collection, Bipolar Lexicon, is available from Unsolicited Press. She serves as a reader for E&GJ Press. Diagnosed with bipolar disorder in her teens, Megan's mission is to inspire others stigmatized for their mental health. She lives in Jacksonville, Florida with her partner of six years, their four-year-old son, and two mollycoddled cats. Her loves include alligators, air hockey, astrology, snorkeling, gardening, and calligraphy.

PANCREATIC CANCER OF THE CHEST AND BONES
STEVE DENEHAN

I see it in your eyes
and I know it sounds crazy
let's just go
we can outrun it

I think

Let us try
I still have youth
have energy
I want to run
but I won't leave you
so come
come now
this night
with me

It will fall from my bones
it will slip from my chest
it will cower and squirm and be gone
black oil in the gutter

Let us go
let us try
we can run toward the sun
so the day never ends

I see it in your eyes
I know it sounds crazy
let's just go

Steve Denehan lives in Kildare, Ireland with his wife Eimear and daughter Robin. He has been published in The First Literary Review, Poets And Poetry, The Opiate, Medusa's Kitchen, Better Than Starbucks and The Poet Community. His poems are to be published in upcoming issues of Sky Island Journal, Fowlpox Press, The Evening Street Press, The Folded Word and Third Wednesday.

THE GENERAL'S CHAIR
JASON BARTLES

The General spots Kitty across the street. From her chair she surveys the outside world and her stories.

"No, it can't be Kitty. She's still buried, and that one's too young," she reasons aloud.

She loosens her oxygen cord and grabs a pen and small notebook from the side table. She bought the notebook at a yard sale the last time she left the house on a cigarette run. Now someone has to smuggle cigarettes through the open window while her husband is away.

On the first page, she wrote numbers from one to fifty. The first seven are scratched out.

The heading reads, "Days without Smoking." Some pages are titled with the names of her relatives and former friends. On others she records details from the Daily about the social problems plaguing the local population. In another section, "Suspicious Events," dated two years ago, she documented the following:

Monday, 14:32. A cat arrives. Brown fur. Jumps across the headstones. Avoids walking on the ground above the deceased. Leaves cemetery, returns the way it came.

Tuesday, 14:37. A cat arrives. Brown fur. Jumps across the headstones. The suspect appears to be the same as the day before. It turns its head toward my window. I stared it dead in its eyes. Then, it leaves.

Wednesday, 14:33. The suspect returns again. Jumps across the headstones. Refuses my stare. Runs after a squirrel and accidentally runs over Mary. Then, it leaves.

Thursday, 14:45. The suspect does not return today.

Friday, 16:00. The suspect does not return today.

This time last year the General detailed her surroundings:

Today, April, approximately four inches of snow have accumulated on the chapel rooftop in a freak snowstorm. The globe's not getting any warmer over here.

The General opens her notebook to a new page, writes the date, and records everything she sees during the commercial break:

A white truck arrives at approximately 12:31. It parks in the middle of the lot just outside the cemetery. The door opens. A suspicious woman gets out. Approximately 5'7". Brown hair. The suspect is wearing a midnight-hussy colored miniskirt, disrespectful, low-cut blouse, and slutty pumps. Climbs chapel stairs. Three knocks. Waits. Three more knocks.

She walks into the cemetery and falls out of sight behind the chapel. Chapel closed for more than five years. Mary was the last one buried in there. Behind chapel only broken headstones and empty bottles according to my last visit. The suspect returns to truck. She appears to be exasperated. Leaves cemetery, returns the way she came.

The local intrigue leaves her almost breathless, but she musters enough energy to title the page "Suspicious Woman" and closes the notebook.

At the base of the foothills everyone calls the Mountains, only two old houses stand across the street from the mid-century chapel. The General and her husband live in one, and a widower, to whom she no longer speaks, lives in the other with his teenage grandson.

There had been plans to build a semi-gated subdivision with tennis courts and a community pool that would have stretched from their backyards to the base of the Mountains. Developing runoff reservoirs masquerading as lakes on formerly wooded quarter-acre lots, for a brief period, proved a lucrative business here.

The orange clay lots now stand empty with small patches of dandelions and prickly weeds spreading where oaks and dogwoods used to blossom. A deep pit floods every time it rains and collects plastic bags and scrap building materials in its center. Disconnected PVC pipes rise from the ground marking what would have been a bathroom, a dishwasher, a sewage drain.

Only two visitors frequent the cemetery since the chapel shuttered its stained glass windows five years ago. When the furniture store in Town was converted into The Hearth, a place of worship with comfy sofas and Lay-Z-Boys in place of splintering pews, even Pastor Eric tired of making the hike out here. Now the Pastor's wife returns once a month to sweep the chapel steps, check the locks on the doors, and remove any litter sticking in the rod-iron fence that stretches across the front of the cemetery, dividing the dearly departed from the gravel lot. Always ignored, Judy smiles and waves as she looks across the street and through the open window to the General sitting in her chair.

Occasionally, the neighbor's grandson mows between the tombstones and makes a quick pass over the General's lawn in exchange for a few cans of beer that she passes him through the window in plain daylight.

After the suspicious woman leaves, the General keeps her eyes trained on the cemetery gates. She places her pen and notebook on the side table next to a full ashtray. She drinks a beer and uses her thesaurus as a coaster so as not to ruin the varnish on the refurbished tables her grandson, Charlie, recently brought her. Looking for the remote she always loses, she searches with her hands under the cushion. She lifts her right side. No remote. Then her left side. Still no. She leans forward to check in the creases behind her but feels a dull sensation between her thighs.

"God dammit. It's always the last place you expect."

Her stories come back on, and she shushes the empty room.

***

"I deserve to be pampered today," she decrees to no one minutes before her stories begin.

She gets up from her chair and reaches for the hose that hangs through the open window. Years ago she used it to water the marigolds and petunias that flowered among creeping weeds along the front of her cement-slab porch. To her surprise, Charlie invented a renewed use for the hose and ripped it from the vines and grasses that had grown through it. She feels light-headed after bending to pick up the hose. She stumbles and something jerks her head to the side. The oxygen cord tightens around her face and its tentacles pull violently against her nostrils.

"Son of a..."

The pain irradiating across her face and into the back of her eyes, not decorum, stops her from finishing the phrase. She leans on the side table to catch her breath, almost spilling her beer, but she tightens her hand around the hose. Standing alone makes her heart rate climb, and the fear of falling with the oxygen cord wrapped around her head beats through her chest like a medieval war drum. Once her stability returns, she leans forward and her knees crack as she bends to untangle the oxygen cord from the other cables behind her chair. The General suffers those minor aches without complaint.

Her grandson also installed a pendant light just above her chair. Now she can read the Daily and finish her crosswords without squinting. "My head is so much clearer at night," she had been hinting to Charlie. "It's so dark in here after dinner," she said another time. "I'd have more time to talk with your aunt, but I can only work on my crosswords in the morning, and she's at work by the time my stories finish," was the phrase that penetrated his thick skull. The following week he was splicing wires and testing a new switch.

Playing puppet master often pleases her more than giving direct orders, though she employs both tactics generously.

The General pulls enough slack from the ball of cables behind her to sit more comfortably. She lifts her legs and pulls the blue lever that extends from the armrest with her left hand while she holds the hose in her right. The lever opens a metal drawer from below the chair where she rests her feet. With the hose aimed at the drawer, she presses the orange button next to the lever to turn on the heating coils. The water always comes out cold, but she endures the discomfort until it warms.

Charlie assured her that it only takes five minutes to heat the water. She sets her stopwatch with the intention of recording the precise time in her notebook. "We'll see about that," she says out loud, hoping for a flaw in this contraption of his.

The heat slowly eases some of the pain in her joints. She rests her head, and the tension around her eyes and in her thoughts loosens. The General thinks of Kitty. They buried her in that tomb two months ago, but they can't possibly let her die now. The General recalls every detail of the plot as the warm water soothes her bony calves. Kitty's daughter, Roxana, desperately wanted to inherit the Caribbean mansion and her grandmother's fortune, which Kitty had been squandering on spa days and chartered flights. But Roxana was not only greedy. She owed a loan shark, the greasy-looking Don DiNero, half a million dollars, which she had used to buy the silence of a reporter who blackmailed her with unseemly photos that proved her affaire de coeur with the town's biracial mayor. The General is as alarmed as Kitty by her daughter's taste in men. Then, Roxana bought a potion from a traveling apothecary and used it to put her mother to sleep. Everyone thought Kitty had died. They buried her sleeping-but-not-dead body the next day. No one knew Roxana had arranged for the casket to be hooked up to air and water tubes, Kitty's only life line. "Murder is not in my veins," Roxana assured the General while looking directly in her eyes.

The five-minute timer sounds and the General turns it off. The water consistently warms well before it beeps, so keeping a record would not prove anything worthwhile. Instead she turns up the volume on the TV. Time passes without much notice. The same commercials blare at her every few minutes. She laughs at the repeated puns and delights in the hard bodies. She inhales deeply as the commercial actors light a cigarette and chooses to join them. When the opening credits start, her heart skips a beat, and she blows a small ring of smoke into the empty room.

"You'll get out of there soon enough, Kitty. Just a little longer, hun," she says. "Today is your day. I feel it in my bones."

The camera opens on Kitty lying on her side in a velvet-lined casket cut lengthwise so the General can see her entire body. The two tubes poke through the casket near her head beside a stash of dehydrated food. Roxana had dated a Russian cosmonaut who provided her with the vacuum-sealed pouches. Kitty's scenes are framed with detail shots of a small green capsule etched with a skull and crossbones tied around her wrist. Roxana had a flair for the dramatic that made her irresistible to foreign men and the General's curious spirit. Through a small speaker in the top of the casket, Roxana communicated with her mother. "If the life I have provided you becomes unbearable," she paused and pursed her lips, "swallow that pill, and you will be forever free."

The General revels in every moment, waiting for the turning point, but the only development today is that Roxana's brother, Elijah, becomes suspicious of Kitty's sudden death.

"Elijah's coming," the General offers her support. "Just breathe, slow and deep. Keep your heart steady."

At the end of the program, the water has cooled around her feet, and her joints tighten. Charlie installed a thirty-minute timer on the heating coils to prevent accidents. Her knees crack as she lifts her legs. Her pulse quickens. She reverses the blue lever, and the spa slides back under the chair, splashing some water on the carpet. A drain clicks open in the bottom of the drawer, and the General hears a trickle in the pipe that leads from her chair through a small hole in the wall below the window to water the empty flowerbed. The General scans the cemetery and parking lot noting that the suspicious woman did not return today. She considers drying her feet with a towel, but it smelled terribly of mold the last time she opened the lower cabinet.

"Best to let them air dry, oh natural."

***

Woken by the sound of her own snoring, the General chokes on the empty space that fills her tattered lungs. The plastic tube had fallen from her nostrils while she slept. She grasps at the cord, pulling and pulling as her heart beats faster, but she only finds more cord. The air she needs barely escapes her as she searches for the opening. She recalls a commercial that explained how the blood carries oxygen through the body and worries that she should have called her doctor about the advertised pills. She finds the opening in the cord, tucks the ends into her nostrils, and wraps its around her ears. The cool air flows down the back of her throat.

Her deep gasps are interrupted by wheezing and coughing for the next half hour as she sips a beer at room temperature. She does not have the strength to turn and take a chilled one from the mini-fridge Charlie installed in one of the cabinets that now extend up and over her chair in a large arch. She cannot even gather the energy in this early summer humidity to search for the remote control that slipped again underneath the cushion. All the General can do is stare at the infomercial for a new plastic box the host claims can cook a whole turkey in less than fifteen minutes. She would have loved to have such an appliance back in the seventies when she woke at dawn to prepare Christmas dinner: honey-glazed ham, scalloped potatoes, green bean casserole, hot rolls, cranberry sauce, punch, sparkling wine, whiskey sours, old-fashioneds, seven and sevens, side cars, and bourbon, neat, no, on the rocks. She delighted in such a decadent touch, sipping icy drinks by the fire in winter. The bourbon cooled and burned as it coated her throat, soothing her from the inside out as it mixed with the bitter smoke that quickened her senses. But now her family members have conspired to prevent her from drinking anything but weak beer, and they avoid stepping on her oxygen cord while reminding her of the flagrant dangers of smoking indoors.

From her chair, the General sees Charlie's wood-paneled station wagon pull into the drive. He sits there for a few minutes talking to himself before opening the door. She watches him walk to the tailgate, open the hatch, and dig through a pile of cables, photocopied manuals, and scraps of wood he gathered from the abandoned lots behind her house.

"He better fix the spa this week," she says in a raspy outburst. Two weeks have passed since she broke the nozzle after throwing it at the window in a fit of impatient rage waiting day in and day out for the suspicious woman to return. The General sits and stares with her notebook in her lap during every commercial. Now she most fears that the woman will return during one of her naps. She has to find out what that woman is all about. No one comes out here anymore, because everyone and everything worth seeing can be found in Town. Only Charlie makes the hike out here, and only on Fridays. "But Charlie's a nobody," she thinks. "Even if he does live in Town."

Charlie pokes his head through the open window.

"TGIF, General," he tries not to mumble as he speaks to her.

"Yeah, get your lazy butt inside."

He still knocks as he opens the front door. The General refuses to leave her chair, but she taught him with a wooden spatula to the hind quarters to never open the door to another person's house without knocking.

"Enter," she grants permission.

He shuts the door too quickly. As it slams, the cabinets surrounding the General's chair wobble and creak under their own weight, but she does not wince or shrug. A picture frame falls from one of the higher shelves. Charlie rushes to pick it up. His fingers leave prints on the greasy, yellowed film that covers the glass and wood and extends over the entire room. The wallpaper, pulling away at the seams, is tinged a brownish gray, and the air tastes of sweat and gunpowder.

"I'd stay longer if it wasn't for that smell," Charlie tells himself. During his drive from his cubicle at the phone company, he plans his retreat. Often he lies to the General, even though she had taught him to respect his elders. "But she hates to be called 'ma'am' since it makes her feel old," he rationalizes, "so no harm done."

This week he can tell the truth. "I can't stay long. I've got a date with John tonight," he explains. They met on a website for single men. He always complains to the General that he has a hard time finding other guys in Town looking for more than a quick release in the backseat of a car. The General starts to respond, but she only coughs.

"Cat got your tongue, General?"

"Shut your..." she chokes on her words. She gets embarrassed when showing a sign of weakness, but she knows how to conceal her emotions. "I don't care how horny you are. The only leaking hose you need to worry about is the one outside my window. It's unacceptable to leave it broken for this long. If you can't take care of this, then I'll call your brother to have him do it."

"Let's see. Today...," he starts to say, relying on experience to ignore her tantrums. He looks around the growing apparatus he has been building to make her more comfortable, searching for a place to connect the next segment. The shelves are piled with paperback crime and romance novels, an incomplete collection of Nancy Drew stories, and the General's prized book, Catcher in the Rye. Used napkins are tucked into a plastic flower arrangement of roses and lilies, and cobwebs cover her ceramic figurines of anthropomorphized cows working on a farm. The cabinet doors no longer close on the sweatshirts, towels, plastic silverware, coffee mugs, playing cards, light bulbs, crushed cans, extension cords, emery boards, scissors, and dirty plates that had been served to the General. An old ashtray now sits alone, enshrined on one shelf, with cigarette butts spilling over the edges. "I can't fix the nozzle. I'll buy a new one and bring it next week. I promise. But today I brought you a computer."

Charlie recently bought a new one for himself and spent hours the night before erasing old files, folders, music, and an impressive collection of erotic photos and videos that he had accumulated over years. Since John asked him out for a second date, he decided not to transfer them. His heart flutters at the thought of John's pompadour and tattoos, but he gets a whiff of the General's breath that turns his stomach.

"Why would I possibly need one of those?"

"So you can get online. I bought you a slot machine game, too."

"I can play that online?"

"Yeah, and the best part is that it's free. You won't lose any money. You always complain about that."

"What's the point then?" she mutters. Watching the reels spin on the video machine used to send a tingling anxiety through her arms, torso, and legs, replacing the touch of her husband after decades of supposedly monogamous cohabitation. But Charlie knew nothing of this. She might have taught him to cuss, but she was not a hussy.

"I'm sure you'll love it once you give it a try."

"No, I quit gambling."

Charlie brings her a boxy, tangerine and white computer and a new shelf with a hinge mechanism that will allow the General to swivel the screen in front of her and push it to the side during her stories. He holds his breath as he digs through the tangled, slimy cords spilling out between the chair and the cabinets. Some he had labeled with masking tape: mini-fridge, spa, radio. But he got lazy once he started putting in the LED lamps and the surround-sound speakers he bought at The Hearth's garage sale. He is not a church-goer, but the General taught him to never pass up a good bargain. The oxygen tube weaves through all the cords and gets more tangled every time the General pulls at it. Mold spreads from the spa around the floor. He considers cleaning this to help with the smell.

"General, it looks like I need a few more screws and hooks than I thought to get this set up today. I'll come back next Friday, untangle everything, clean a bit, and get your computer up and running."

"What do you mean you can't finish it today? And the spa?"

"Can't you just take a bath?" His body freezes at the sound of his own voice. The General's face turns flush with rage, and she scrunches her forehead. She is about to curse him but loses her reeking breath. "I, um, just, with the heat, it might help your breathing. General, oh, please, take a deep breath. You just need to relax."

He grabs her a cold beer from the mini-fridge with his jittery hand. Then he goes out to his car to bring in a case of beer to restock while she catches her breath.

"And here's a few cigs, too, but don't tell anyone, ok? Can I get you anything else, General?"

She shakes her head and stares him in the eyes.

"I'll see you next week and fix everything up. Just one week, but I have to get going now."

He kisses her oily cheek, turns to the door, eager to wash the dank smell from his body and forget his unplanned assault. He takes a deep breath once he steps outside and lights a cigarette. The General glares as he climbs into his car and drives away.

"Jack ass," she spits the words. She takes another sip as the same infomercial begins for the third time today. She pulls down the makeup mirror attached to the cabinet overhead and wipes off his kiss with her Redskins t-shirt. "I'll take a bath tomorrow," she says to herself.

***

"I had always knew that girl was trouble."

"She was so shy in school."

"Jen graduated with you?"

"No, she was a year behind me."

"That was a bad year all around."

"What do you mean?"

"First, them Inner City transplants lit the Christmas tree on fire. And there were how many teen pregnancies that year? At least three. All because they stopped teaching proper etiquette to young ladies so there was time to teach you kids how to wrap a dick in a condom. It's not rocket science, you know. Serves them morons right."

The General lets the hiss of the beer can linger as she opens it, leaning forward so Charlie can screw the scraps of metal to the wobbling cabinets and affix them to the wall. After a terrible dream in which the entire slimy stand, tangled in oversized roses and lilies, crashed and buried the General in a heap of rubble, he decided to expand and stabilize the apparatus. In recent weeks, he fixed the spa, untangled and cleaned the mildewed cords, vacuumed, disinfected every surface in the room, and installed the computer. He plans to attach new sections to both sides of the existing cabinets on digital, hydraulic hinges, along with a new computer tray, that the General can control with her customized remote. Then she will be able to swing the microwave, coffee maker, mini-fridge, or pantry sections within reach of her chair and avoid exhausting trips to the kitchen between the infrequent visits of her extended family members. With a hose that attaches to the bathroom tub down the hallway, he ran water lines for an ice maker and a small sink, and thick, orange extension cords now form a network connecting to every outlet in the house to avoid overloading the living room circuits.

"It's a bunch of mongoloids running the School Board these days."

"Mongoloids?" The General's offensive vocabulary seizes new territory with the daring of a guerrilla cell. Either it was a tactic recovered from the decades before his birth, or she had unearthed the word in her thesaurus for her puzzles. Charlie considers confronting the General's attack, but as always he chooses to remain silent.

"But that Jen girl, well, there are no words for her." The General always stands at the vanguard, sussing out past and present minutiae from the lives of those downtown residents without revealing her sources of information.

"She brought it on herself," Charlie explains between the sounds of the power drill. "I have no patience for people like that."

"What the girl needed was a smack on the ass when she was little."

"I heard that the money came from an older gentleman she was seeing on the side. Got him to sign over his will before his mysterious accident."

"That. Little. Hussy," she audibly punctuates her judgment.

"And that he thought she needed some help to pay for her mother's medical expenses, but that old bag died years ago."

"Watch your tongue. Dear, old Lillian, may she rest in peace. She's buried across the street you know. Third row back on the right side."

"Then again, the old guy clearly got something out of the arrangement, too. I can't imagine sleeping with someone who could be my grandfather."

"Well, if he buys you nice things, you might change your mind."

"Maybe for a new car."

"Or a house."

"Or a trip to Maine in the spring."

"I don't know about no Maine. You know what they say about those yanks up North. That..."

"They say the seafood is delicious," he interrupts her, "right off the coast, because of the cold water coming down from Canada or the North Pole or something. Lobsters as big as your face. But that's my dream. What did the boys used to do to get your interest?"

"Back in my day, you know, things were simpler. If a man tucked in his shirt, bought you dinner and dessert, maybe even a night cap, then you knew you had to repay the expense."

"Come on, General, I can't imagine you going along with that."

"Times were different then. A guy willing to do all that would get your engine running. And compared to all the guys who thought a good date was to get a beer at the Corner."

"Some things have not changed then."

"Don't tell me John took you to the Corner."

"No, not there. But it was our six-month anniversary, and all we did was have a few drinks and burgers and fall asleep on the couch back home."

"Hun, there's nothing to complain about there."

"I guess."

"Trust me. Someone's who's happy just being in your company is a keeper. I have to make your granddaddy stay back in his room when he's home all day. Otherwise, I never get no peace around here."

The conversation comes to a lull as they approach their own insecurities, and Charlie finishes attaching the last support beam. He gives the whole apparatus a shove with his hands. Then he walks to the front door, opens and slams it, but the fortified cabinets stand firm during the assault. The General observes the craftsmanship. She purses her lips as her eyes dart from corner to corner, nodding ever so slightly. Charlie understands her silence as thorough approval of a job well done.

"That should do it. They're not going anywhere now. I'll be back tomorrow to work on the remote control so you don't have to get up every time you want something."

"Are you hungry?"

"I haven't ate yet."

The General leans forward to pull the freezer cabinet toward her. The microwave cabinet is above it and also slides easily within her reach. She almost compliments Charlie on the design. She chooses a frozen French bread pepperoni pizza, opens the plastic wrapper, pulls out the pizza, and places the cardboard holder with the shiny base into the microwave for six minutes. Charlie tidies his tools and takes the unused scrap metal back to his car.

When he returns, the General has already begun to cut the pizza. The smell of meat and soggy bread mixes with the hot breeze flowing through the open window. She gives up on the dull knife, grabs the pizza with both hands, and rips it in two. She plucks at the melted mozzarella strings until the halves are completely separated and hands one to Charlie. He tries not to think about how long it has been since she washed her hands, but he finds comfort knowing that now she has a sink, hand soap, and a dryer right next to her.

"Next I want you to get me a toilet under the cushion here and a trashcan. The bathroom's too far."

"Yes, General."

***

Kitty remains buried alive for another day. When her stories end, the General grabs the remote attached to a stretch, spiraling cord and shuts off the TV. She presses the yellow button to command the computer to slide in front of her. A fan whirrs in the base of the tray as it approaches.

The General follows a strict regimen when surveying the net. At precisely fifteen hundred hours she opens the Daily's website for her briefing. The cover story reports to her the time and location of the annual Christmas tree lighting ceremony. She sets a reminder in her calendar for next week. The only time she attended the kids were crying in the icy air, so they left before the ceremony began. She made hot cider for them all at home to reconcile yet another in a long string of holiday disappointments and spiked her own mug with bourbon. After analyzing the official reports, she scrolls to the top of the page and clicks on the Tattler tab to better understand how things look on the ground.

Before the Daily was forced to cut back its print run, readers called a toll-free number to leave an anonymous comment on any aspect of local or national news. Most citizens accepted the burden of correcting misinformation provided by their fellow Tattlers, as the informants were generally called. A minimum-wage earning teenager had thirty minutes to listen to the recordings and select which ten would appear in print before moving on to make an educated guess at the local weather report. The rule of thumb was that it was usually two or three degrees cooler than in Baltimore, usually a bit sunnier or a bit cloudier, depending on the teen's mood and disposition. The small staff was not to be bothered with such trivial details. And Tattlers who complained about the inaccurate weather reports were never to be published.

The General scours the Tattler section of the website with her verbal red pen. She has perfected a system for analyzing the comments that flood the running feed. She always works backward from the most recent comments and maintains records of the most salient details, filed in various folders on her desktop, in case she needs to cross-check facts or confirm suspicions about the identity of the Tattlers and of those sick-minded individuals whose improper behaviors are righteously broadcast across Town.

14:39:03 To those of you who want school to be all year: I may be alone on this one, but if they decide to have school all year, I will not send my child. I happen to love my child.
The General files this both under "school board" and "debbie s."

14:14:48 To the transplants: We are tired of you trying to change things around here. It was perfectly fine the way it was. If you don't like it here, then go back where you came from.

"This town's going to shit." She picks up the lit cigarette from the ashtray and takes a slow drag. The smoke flaps her lungs like an American flag in the heat of battle. She judges the comment unworthy of archiving, because of its hasty generalizations, though not in protest at the content. "Logic must prevail in such trying times."

13:30:41 To those of you who don't support the so-called George W. Bush War: I want to know if you support President Obama sending an additional 21,000 troops to Afghanistan to fight a country that hasn't done anything to us.

"Them poor boys getting sent to be blown up in the desert. Things were simpler in my day," she meditates as she files these facts to "war crimes." She flicks the ash from the end of the cigarette and sets it down.

13:22:32 To the guy who runs around town on his Segway: you need to follow traffic rules like everyone else. He runs out into the middle of the intersection and refuses to go around people on the sidewalks. He almost ran over my child. What are our taxes paying for if not public safety?

"Charlie almost ran him over once, the stupid porker. Too fat and lazy to just walk like everyone else," she says. She also files this to "debbie s."

12:57:02 To the Gothic-looking lady in Town who yelled at my children in the grocery store: I wrote down your license plate and it is being turned in to the local authorities.

"I'd have smacked her in her damn face. Goth freak!" The General would have added this complaint to the mounting evidence she has been acquiring on the Goths in Town, but her rage incites another coughing fit. The color drains from her face as she leans forward and shoves the computer tray, but the whirring fans resist her. A memory of Mary flashes across the General's mind. Mary used to wear frilly summer dresses and carry pitchers of lemonade on decorative platters to serve her husband and son on a hot summer day in their manicured backyard. The General's prime directive was to remind Mary of her imperfections. She practiced stealth to pluck roses and lilies from her bushes in the middle of the night, and she blamed

Mary for the slugs that infested her back porch. But the General had the pleasure of laughing into Mary's grave while tossing a bucket of dirt and salted slugs onto her casket to demonstrate that she had won their on-going war.

Now she gasps for the thick air that flows through her oxygen cord. Her lungs relax with time, and she orders the mini-fridge to swing within reach. Hydraulic pumps hiss in obedience preempting the sound of the pull-tab can. She reclines her chair and allows the beer to soothe her inflamed throat. With another click of her remote, the lights in the aquarium above her head flicker. Only one betta fish remains in the green-brown water.

She wonders if it is dead. Then it swims toward the glass bottom of the tank almost looking at the General in the eyes. Thoughts of Charlie's face recoiling from her verbal assault flood her memory. "You needed to hear the truth about John," she told him. But he plugged in the water filter, his final addition to the apparatus that now fills the room, and walked out the front door, softly pulling it closed behind him. He did not look at her through the window as he drove away. The General considers making note of another Friday alone in her computer files, but instead she takes another drink and turns off the tank's light.

She tosses the crumpled can toward the trash bin built into one of the many cabinets of different colors and stains. It bounces off the overflowing pile and lands among the newly mildewing plates, napkins, and cans that carpet the floor in the spots where the cabinets do not slide in and out of place. With the remote in her hand, she sits up in the chair, leans to the side using her forearm to lift her bottom from the cushion, and presses the red button. The cushion slides back behind the chair with the sound of an airlock door that opens onto a toilet. The General almost collapses onto the seat, and little by little she pushes her burgundy sweatpants past her bony knees. An acrid smell fills the General's nostrils as urine trickles into the basin. Instinctually she tries to hold her breath, but that only makes her wheeze and gasp for more air than can flow through her oxygen cord. She sits like this concentrating once more on her breathing until she gains enough strength to press the white flush button, lift herself, and press the red button to make the seat cushion return to its place.

By now, the winter sun has set. The computer light illuminates only her withered face in the dark room. The General commands the cabinets to encase her frail body in her chair and turns on the space heaters. She reclines, adjusts the oxygen cord, and her breathing and heart rate slow as the computer screen fades to black.

***

By noon the next day, blocks of sunlight advance across the floor, rise and fall over crumpled cans and cardboard boxes, and climb the makeshift fort. Imperfections in the design have left small openings in the outer wall of cabinets, the General's arrow loops, as Charlie defended them to his grandmother. Around noon sunbeams break through the barrier, and one pierces the General's closed eyelids. She tries to shift from the line of fire, but the oxygen cord holds her head in place. She winces in the blinding light.

"God..." she mutters before the coughing seizes her body. She reaches for the oxygen cord to release the tension and sits up in her chair. This fit was briefer than most. Shrouded by the cabinets, her eyes adjust to the semi-darkness crisscrossed by rays of sun light. She turns to the coffeemaker and fills a stained mug. The caffeine pumps blood and oxygen through her veins, reinvigorating her to start her morning duties.

She grabs the remote and commands the cabinets to withdraw from her chair. The hydraulic pumps hiss as the walls part and reveal the General to the midday light. Then she orders the window open to cleanse the ripe air while the heaters remain on full blast. The computer tray whirrs toward her with another click of the remote, and she enters her password with her pointer fingers certain that no one can bypass her security measures. On her desktop, she right-clicks the file named "charlie." Because of a sudden cough, she accidentally clicks on Move to Trash instead of Open. She swiftly counters by opening the Trash icon to restore her document but, to her surprise, uncovers a massive archive of deleted files.

"Rookie mistake, Charlie! It's my lucky day," she says with delight. The General's dry mouth almost waters as she begins to comb through the secrets and mysteries her grandson intended to hide from her.

Never distracted from her priorities, she pauses to turn on her stories. "Maybe it'll be Kitty's lucky day, too." For weeks the General's stories have been framed with brief scenes of Kitty breaking through the wooden casket and tunneling her way toward the surface.

The General, more efficient than ever, closely monitors the unfolding drama of her stories while she digs, during commercial breaks, through Charlie's digital skeletons. The files at the top are named with random numbers and letters. She clicks through images of cats and dogs and witticisms. She finds elegant bathrooms and kitchens that mix vintage chairs with modern tables, sleek appliances with frumpy textiles. She skims outdated technical manuals that explain the basics of html and how to build a home radio. The General would not be swayed from her task no matter the quantity of her grandson's inane interests. She relies on her conviction that this painstaking work will bear the sweet results she needs to lure Charlie back to her side, even if only through blackmail, but until then, she can rely on Roxana's flamboyant Caribbean lover to entertain her.

A curious video file offers itself to the General. The camera comes into focus on a thirty-something man's square jaw and stubble before panning down his shaved chest. It lingers on his upper torso that rocks gently from the motion of his right arm. He flexes his abdominal muscles for her and lifts his hips into view of the camera.

The General feels a warmth that slowly eases some of the pain in her hips and joints.

"What kind of filth is this?" she says as she rests her head. The tension around her eyes and in her thoughts loosens as the camera returns to the man's eyes. The General ignores the plotline of her stories as sensation returns to her aching thighs. She takes a slow, deep drag on her oxygen and exhales audibly. A light, fetid cough escapes her lips. Her hands caress the arm rests on her chair, against her will, and she scratches the fabric with her nails as the camera pulls back to reveal the naked man's body sitting in a black leather recliner. They stare one another in the eyes. She sneaks another look as he performs for her pleasure alone. The commercials blare throughout the room, but she only notices the sound of his quickening breath. Her eyes flutter between open and closed, and the General's joints almost melt into her chair as her hands glide across the fabric of her sweatshirt.

"Excuse me, ma'am, do you know who takes care of the...." The suspicious woman stops mid-sentence. She stares through the open window in amazement at the enormous contraption and piles of trash that fill the General's living room, unaware of the General's startled reaction.

"Do you need a lawyer?" the television inquires.

The General's body snaps back into its rundown order. The color drains from her flush face and, with every dragging second, embarrassment turns to fury.

"You! You... perverted hussy!" The General grabs the spa hose hanging from a hook near the sink, raises it in both hands, aims with perfection toward the suspicious woman's face, and opens fire. She blasts the makeup from her over-painted face, and the General proceeds methodically to drench her intruder's pea coat and heavy slacks. When she can no longer see a dry spot of fabric, skin, or hair, she releases the handle in mercy.

The suspicious woman wipes her face and leaves a dripping trail in the frost as she runs across the street to the parking lot.

"That's right, run, you sick freak!" the General shouts through the window. The trembling woman climbs back in her truck. She leaves skid marks outside the cemetery as she returns the way she came. "I better never see you around these..." she yells before her lungs pull her back in her chair. She gasps and chokes and watches helplessly as the man on her computer reaches his final climax and Kitty's slender fingers break through the cemetery grass.

Jason A. Bartles is a writer, translator, and Assistant Professor of Spanish at West Chester University of Pennsylvania. He holds a PhD from the University of Maryland, College Park, in Latin American literatures and cultures. His website can be found at: https://jasonabartles.wordpress.com/

THE QUILPRY
KOBINA WRIGHT

They were growing distressed and irritable. They hadn't been fed in four days. The one called Ledford managed to climb the wire fence on the cage door and get to the single light bulb on the ceiling. He had unscrewed it after it had been turned off and cooled, then crunched down on it between his large teeth, slicing his tongue and gums, leaving a spatter of blood on the cement floor. It was an act of protest; however, they all had to sit in the dark now.

Ledford ate a lightbulb. To Trung this meant the quilpry were impervious to pain – categorically dangerous. He was arriving at this conclusion even without Ledford's stunt. The binder didn't mention glass... or light bulbs. He wouldn't go back in the cage to replace it. They were out of tranquilizers.

Trung hadn't seen them in four days and felt responsible to check on them and when he peeked around the corner into the cage, he trembled and leaned heavily on his crutch, inhaling through his nose... exhaling through his mouth. He could smell that their cage had not been cleaned in a while. Their silver bodies were slumped like snow heaps on the floor. The door surely alerted them to his presence but he tried to stay quiet, not wanting to get caught watching them openly.

They had real thoughts. Not like dogs. Like dolphins. He knew it. Their pale teal, cat-like eyes bore through him like screws, reaching the molten colors of his insecurities, despite the brave front. Their shimmering ape-like arms folded across their chests in his presence, and he knew from recent experience that if close enough, one would impale him with the short horn that protruded from its head.

It wasn't the violence that kept Trung hidden. He was afraid of their eyes. In the beginning, he and his brother used to talk to them regularly, like pets. They gave the quilpry names that the creatures never responded to. Their eyes were flat, but intelligent. When they stared at the brothers, Trung felt... judged. He sensed their arrogance and analytics, right there in those teal cat eyes.

The quilpry showed no excitement at the attention they were given and often outright ignored Trung and his brother – unless there was food. When food was involved, three adult males came to the door of the cage – methodically, their height reaching the brothers' waists when the creatures' hands and feet were on the ground. When the three stood upright, they stared the brothers squarely in the eyes, looking neither friendly nor unfriendly. The three always stood. The females, slightly smaller, rarely stood as far as the brothers could tell but did stare. The babies, twin males, never left their mother and even they stared.

"Sleep tight." Trung's brother would say before walking away from the cage. After the tranquilizers wore off and the quilpry had eaten their dinner, his brother would flip the light switch with a hard click, leaving them all in darkness. Sleep tight.

Once, Trung had lingered around the corner of the cage near the door, out of sight of the creatures, wallowing in self-pity about being there at home, friendless and lonely while his brother and a group of his brother's friends made plans to run wild in the city. They were at the brothers' house at that moment, drinking and laughing about things that were only funny to them, preparing to head out. Trung had only been invited two awkward times into the city with them and later pretended not to care that he was never invited again. He alone served the creatures then and was about to open the door leading outside the enclosure when he halted. He heard one of the quilpry nasally parrot his brother. Sleep tight. This was followed by a soft cackling sound from the cage. That could not have been the hushed sounds of laughter. Giggling. These creatures, always silent and unresponsive, were mocking them. Talking! Trung hurriedly ran back around the corner to peer into the cage but they had stopped and were as stoic as when he'd left them.

Trung excitedly relayed the incident back at the house. His brother, grimacing and sucking his teeth, threatened to lock him up with the creatures, then drunkenly cursed him, calling him an idiot in front of everyone. Trung knew better. His brother didn't really think he was an idiot. It was a show for his friends.

"No dude. Let's go see. What if your brother's telling the truth? Then who'd be the idiot?"

Trung's brother's friend Glen wanted to witness Trung's wild claim for himself. He stared at Trung a moment, then back at Trung's brother. Three other guys in the room laughed at Trung's brother and voiced their versions of excuses Trung's brother would make if what Trung said was true.

Sorry I didn't believe you Trung, I'm actually dumber than these monkey-catacorns.

Sorry Trung, for calling you an idiot, I'm just an asshole crackhead.

"We gotta see this! Are you kidding me?" A girl, whose name Trung had a hard time remembering (Kimpia or Kimminie or... something) was usually quiet but obviously curious enough to back up Glen.

The group of of six stumbled loudly into the pink graffittied kennel, shushing each other and giggling. Trung's brother turned on the light with a loud thick click and the group of humans stared at the quilpry. Trung's brother's friends who had all seen the creatures, but only once before, were still awed and quite afraid of their strangeness. The quilpry stared back at them.

"What did you say they said? Sleep tight?" Glen asked Trung.

Trung nodded.

One of Trung's brother's friends shouted, "SLEEP TIGHT?"

Trung's brother hissed a warning about yelling at the creatures. He had been terrified of the idea of bringing the group into the pink graffittied kennel again but gave into the surmounting pressure. If Trung would have thought it through, he wouldn't have told his brother about what had happened while his brother's friends were around. He should've waited.

The quilpry said nothing. Trung thought they looked hostile, like people looked when they were trying to control their anger. No amount of prompting or cage kicking or pleasantly spoken insults offered like sugar cubes, made them react to the humans. After a few minutes, the adult quilpry looked away dismissively and only the twin babies continued to stare. Trung half expected the mother to turn the twins' heads away from them. She didn't.

As the group of six left the pink graffittied kennel, Glen patted Trung on the shoulder. The unexpected physical contact made Trung flinch.

"They didn't want to talk to us Trung. I guess they only trust you."

He wanted to, but Trung didn't tell his brother that when it was dark, before he reached the pink graffitted kennel door, he sometimes heard noises. Conversations... Sometimes arguing. Sometimes whispering. They were communicating with each other but not in a language he recognized.

The twins were babies, still on their mother's swollen teats when Trung and his brother stole the crates off a rig. One day, while they waited in stillness together smoking under a patch of trees on the side of the road, hoping for day-labor work, they watched a truck driver drive up and abandon his rig in the sparsely occupied parking lot of a motel in search of entertainment by demure company. They looked at each other. The rig was full of crates but the brothers only stole the ones marked "chairs," "table," "living room," and "electric oven." Trung's brother believed the unmarked rig was from a wholesale furniture store or maybe a moving truck for some wealthy family relocating. They went giddy when they found that all the crates could be moved with just a dolly, conveniently tucked inside by the rig's cargo door and moved quickly to load the crates into their own truck. It took two trips.

They cracked open the plywood crates and stood stunned as they starred at a heap of breathing monkey-unicorn-cat creatures, clearly tranquilized. They moved the boxed creatures carefully, using only their lean muscles and the dolly, depositing them in the abandoned, pink graffitied kennel on their property. The building once housed Cavalier King Charles Spaniels when they stole four purebreds and decided to get into the short-lived business of dog breeding.

Water leaked throughout the pink graffitied kennel when it rained, which was often, but the open community space behind the fenced cage stayed dry. That's where the quilpry went. Seven altogether. Their legs and arms were twisted and looped like silver pretzels while they slept.

The brothers took careful inventory of the rest of their stolen goods. Four hundred tranquilizer darts. One tranquilizer gun. Liquid vitamins in an clear acrylic box with amber vials, syringes, tiny spoons and a white powder Trung discovered, by accident, was confectioners' sugar. There was also a five inch binder labeled "Quilpry" which held general instructions to their daily care, notes on their mating habits, diet, grooming and social behavior. After caring for them for about a month, Trung's brother decided that most of the information in the binder was useless.

The brothers considered breeding and selling the creatures like they had the dogs, but the eldest realized the quilpry were far too unique to sell locally. The umbrella of commonplaceness, essential to pull such a thing off, was absent. They'd cook under the exposure, and whomever they stole the creatures from would easily march the authorities into the pink graffitied kennel and send the young men to prison. His brother wanted to, then, tranquilize the whole lot and dump them. The quilpry. Trung, however, quickly pointed out the danger in that, so took on the bulk of responsibility for the caring of them until... Until. He followed the directions in the binder and tranquilized them before setting out their food – cooked mice, rats or squirrels and served raw vegetables. Under Trung's care it was usually rats and lettuce since rats were the easiest to find and trap and lettuce was cheap. He carefully folded the vitamins into their food and lightly dusted it with confectioners' sugar, assuming it was for masking the strong vitamin taste that every living creature seemed to be repelled by.

Four days ago, low on supplies, Trung decided against tranquilizing them. They liked him better. He always thought they'd been passive with him until he was promptly impaled in the leg when he entered the cage. His brother, a short distance outside the pink graffitied kennel, heard his screams and pulled him out by the armpits. The wound throbbed and spiked; throbbed and spiked, on the ride to the hospital. He had vomited all over himself because the pain had been so intense. Trung told the attending doctor that he'd been stabbed in a fight over a girl.

With what?

His brother had said he'd take care of the quilpry while Trung convalesced, his fighting-over-a girl leg elevated with pillows, back at the house. His brother had slacked off though, and Trung knew it. Selfish fucker. Running around with his friends in the city. He hadn't seen him in three days and Trung himself hadn't been in a hurry to feed the quilpry, still pissed about his leg. They needed to be taught a lesson... and he was scared.

It was impossible to see all the quilpry from where he stood peeking around the corner near the door inside the pink graffitied kennel, especially since there was no longer a light in the cage. Trung could clearly see one of them. It was the one they called Ledford. He and Trung made eye contact and Ledford simultaneously put a foot (or hand) forward, inching a bone behind him in the darkness. Trung's heart thudded in his chest and he wished to God his brother would drag his lazy ass back. It wasn't fair and they were out of tranquilizers.

Kobina Wright created the Hodaoa-Anibo language – a language she views as a work of art, dedicated Africans who were forced to give up their native tongues when once they were enslaved in the New World.

STOPPING AT VINNIE'S ROADSIDE
LAWRENCE F. FARRAR

In the summer of 1980, my tech company dispatched me to Okinawa for a few weeks work with one of our defense contractors. They inadvertently put me up in a seedy hotel located on Kakazu Heights. My room was sparsely furnished and poorly lighted. Thumb-sized geckos scampered across the walls.

As I peered down from my window on that first day, the windswept fields below the hotel struck me as uncultivated and desolate. On an island where every parcel of arable land demanded cultivation, the fact puzzled me. When I asked the manager, Mr. Ueda, about this seeming anomaly, he became hesitant and evasive.

Round-faced and shaven-headed, Ueda was a smallish man, who maintained a Chaplinesque mustache. I learned later he'd been a soldier in the great 1945 battle. That and the fact he hailed from mainland Japan left me perplexed; why had he chosen to live in Okinawa?

In due course, things began to come together. This area below our hilltop hotel had been the site of one of many horrendous battles during the 1945 American fight to take Okinawa. Although the official recovery of remains had concluded years before, mainlanders and Okinawans alike still periodically sifted the soil seeking the bones of those who had died in that cataclysmic conflict. Mr. Ueda told me he'd committed himself to assisting those engaged in that task. Bone-collectors regularly patronized his hotel.

I found the whole business of collecting bones unsettling. Staring out across that field from my window, especially at night, launched chills coursing down my spine. I soon ascertained from Ueda, however, that searching the field for any remains they might unearth and bringing them home to mainland Japan had long been a passion for veterans, survivors, family members, and others. They sought to honor and console the spirits of those who had fallen. In the minds of the collectors, the war had not ended. Finding remains constituted unfinished business. Ueda's exposition made the retrieval activities more understandable.

Still, there also were what at first seemed strange goings-on at a hill-top shrine not far from my hotel. Save for the sound of their shuffling feet, people proceeded silently to and from the shrine along a nearby road. Lanterns flickered in the night, and I could hear what I assumed to be people praying for the war dead. I also discovered that several Okinawan family tombs existed on the side of the hill, not far from our building. Perhaps I was being uncharitable, but, at least for the uninitiated, it proved to be an eerie and unsettling mix.

On occasion, lights in the fields below the hotel captured my attention. I initially assumed them to be associated with Marines from a nearby base conducting night maneuvers. I was damn certain I made out a shadowy column of men marching along the perimeter of the field. I was equally convinced I heard voices and the muffled sound of weapons being fired.

When I checked with Marine Headquarters, however, an empty-faced young captain assured me there had been no maneuvers in the area. He said, "Sir, they say you run into all sorts of things on the island, if you stay here long enough." He smiled and shrugged his shoulders as if to say, but we know better than that, don't we?

What did he know?

So, I again spoke to Mr. Ueda. I wondered if, instead of Marine training, these phenomena could be traced to bone collectors carrying on their excavations, even at night.

"Oh, no sir," Mr. Ueda told me. "They do not work at night. What you see are the spirits of American and Japanese soldiers fighting to capture or defend this hill."

He spoke with absolute sincerity.

"Really, Mr. Ueda? Really?" I delivered a you're putting me on look.

"No, sir. Is true. Ghosts."

Mr. Ueda said Japanese people believed those who died a natural death joined their ancestral spirits. But those who died by violent means had difficulty making the final passage to the spirit world; they were destined to roam the earth. They no longer belonged to the world but were tied to it and reluctant to leave. The collectors provided consolation to the spirits. Even carrying home a bone fragment or a tooth, Ueda said, could help give the spirits peace, help them rest.

Ueda's explanations seemed inconsistent and hard to follow. Maybe it was his broken English; perhaps my imperfect grasp of local lore. In any case, the whole business troubled me. Could I be the only one?

Soon after my arrival, a work assignment took me to the northern end of the island. I promptly wrapped up the job and intended an immediate return trip, even though a typhoon was bearing down on us. Nonetheless, I opted to drive back to Kakazu Heights. As I set out, gusts of wind already whipped palm trees back and forth, and the soggy air threatened to dump sheets of windshield inundating rain. People with good sense had taken shelter at home, and the military bases had buttoned up. Black clouds roiled through a dirty green sky. Ignoring all the warning signs, with confidence bred of ignorance, I calculated the fifty-mile run should be manageable.

I'd made a flawed choice. As I squelched my way south, rain pummeled the car and devoured the beams of my headlights. The road hid from me, as if imposing punishment for my foolishness. Wind gusts tried to push me off course. With no idea of where I was, I barely crept along. Not surprisingly, I hadn't seen another vehicle for twenty minutes, and an overwhelming drowsiness enveloped me.

Fearing I might nod off, I decided to pull over to the side of the road and grab a bit of sleep.

My recollection is unclear, but it must have been at that moment, through the murk, I spotted vague yellow lights. I assumed them to be from a bar or restaurant. Whatever sort of establishment it might be, I needed to stop. The place offered a safe haven, and I drove into the parking lot. Awash in splashing water, the lot stood deserted. Any customers had no doubt long since headed for home. Squinting through the downpour, I made out a sputtering neon sign: Vinnie's Roadside.

I scrambled through the rain, pushed open a set of double doors, and stepped inside. In the muted amber light, I could not determine if the place was open for business. As I brushed away rain drops from my sleeves and shoulders, it seemed the dampness of the storm had permeated the building's interior. And a vague smell of disinfectant, like that in a hospital, laced the air. A scrim of something unknown encircled the place, something palpable enough to make me hesitate.

As my eyes adjusted, I could see a bartender behind the bar. I also made out two elderly men slouched at the end of the bar. A third man sat at a shadowed corner table. They all wore civilian clothing.

The ambience unwelcoming, I felt uncomfortable. Perhaps this was predictable, since I was both wet and tired. Although I'd found refuge from the storm, I experienced an unexplained compulsion to turn back. I dismissed the feeling and claimed a seat halfway up the bar.

The bartender took his time in coming to take my order. An unsmiling and washed out-looking white guy with avian eyes, he struck me as one of those ex-GIs you often found in places like this. Derelicts and left-behinds, they'd stayed on after their service ended and now scraped out a living on the fringes of the military community. I suspect working as a bartender or in some similar employment provided a comfortable milieu for such people. This person would never be going back to the States.

Hands on the bar, he leaned forward in front of me. "What'll it be?"

"I really need a cup of coffee, but is that . . .?

"No coffee. This ain't no restaurant."

When I hesitated, he drummed his fingers on the counter.

"Okay. I'll have a beer and a bag of those chips."

"We're going to close soon," the bartender said. "Storm's gonna hit full force any time now."

"Yeah. I understand. Just came down from up north. It's tough driving."

I can only describe Vinnie's as a guttering place. The grimy bar cried out for a wipe-down. The floor longed for a mop and a broom. The mirror behind the bar, so badly smeared I could not see my reflection, demanded cleaning. The beer arrived with no label and was both tepid and tasteless.

The bartender nodded to the two elderly customers from the end of the bar as they drifted past us. Expressionless, their mood dreary, they said not a word and went out into the rain. I'd sensed an aura of indescribable heaviness about them. To my mortal eyes, they seemed almost like residents of purgatory.

Watching them leave, I knew I, too, should also be on my way; indeed, the storm could only get worse. Yet, I lingered, apprehension tempered by curiosity.

"Who is the guy in the corner?" I asked the bartender. In the vague light, I could barely make out his shadowed form.

"Him? He only comes in once in a while. Usually late in the evening. He's like me. Served his time and stayed here on the Rock. We just call him the Sergeant Major."

When I turned my head in the man's direction, he raised his hand and beckoned for me to join him.

Again, I felt I should be on my way. But, as if someone had gripped my shoulder and drawn me toward him, I experienced an urge to hear what the fellow might have to say. I stepped away from the bar.

"You're wasting your time," the bartender said. "You'll probably think he's looney. Lots of war stories."

"Well, I'm curious."

"Don't say I didn't tell you. Anyway, I'm closing up in in twenty minutes."

I made my way to the corner table.

The Sergeant Major gestured for me to sit down.

I pulled up a wooden chair. "Kind of dark in here," I said. It took a moment to discern his features.

"Way I like it," he said, without further explanation.

Like the two men who'd left, he seemed old, very old. His gray-white hair was cropped short against his skull and framed a leathery, surfeited face. He had dark, deep-set eyes, which he fixed on me as if I were some sort of a curiosity.

He wore a long-sleeved khaki shirt, buttoned to the very top. Scrawny wrists protruded from his shirt cuffs. Resting on the table, his hands drew my attention. The fingers were thin, bony, and the back of his hands wrinkled, with prominent veins.

"You a first timer?" he said. He had a husky, almost rasping, voice.

Uncertain of his meaning, I said, "Yes. I haven't been in here before."

"I mean here on the island. Look too young to know all that went on. The battle. You know. The battle."

I smiled inwardly. I'd been warned.

"Well, I've read some books and talked to some . . ."

"But you weren't in it." He waved his hand dismissively.

"No, sir. I wasn't in it."

"I was in it. You've got no idea what it was like. No idea."

"I understand it was terrible. Heavy casualties."

"Not even close, sonny. Ain't no words for it. None."

I noticed his empty glass. "Could I get you a beer," I said.

He ignored my question. "Japs was up on them ridge lines. Had us in their field of fire. We'd go charging up. They'd come charging back. Nothing there for anybody but a filthy death."

"I can't imagine what it was like."

"No. I expect you can't. Noise. Noise that tore at your ears. Machine guns cackling away. Mortars whooping. Artillery shells whining. Thought you might die just from the noise."

As he recalled it all, I wasn't certain he even knew I was there.

"It got worse day after day. Rained a lot," he said. "You'd jump in a shell hole and find out you was sharing it with parts of dead soldiers. Couldn't tell if they was ours or theirs; maybe both. All mingled together and rotting in the mud. Can't forget the stench. Got all over you."

His gory account repelled me. Still, I sat transfixed as he narrated detail after detail of the fighting, much of which, it turned out, involved efforts to seize the top of Kakazu Heights, the very place I was staying. He'd clearly told the story many times. Nonetheless, he seemed to relive the experience, as if for the first time.

When he finished, he leaned back, and sat quietly, as if relieved to have unburdened himself.

"An amazing story," I said. "Thanks for sharing it." I suppose it sounded like a dorky response.

He nodded. "Too many folks ignorant about what went on here. Needs telling."

"What brings you out on a night like this?" I asked.

"Here on TDY. Always come out when there's a typhoon coming."

His answer puzzled me. "TDY? I don't understand."

"Temporary duty. With a special unit. We help the teams looking for remains uncovered by the storm. We were here. Know the field." He paused. "We owe it to our buddies." Almost as an afterthought, he said, "A lot of them didn't make it."

I know I looked incredulous. His explanation sounded like something I had heard about the Japanese bone collectors. "I thought our government finished its recovery years ago," I said.

"Lots of things people don't know, Sonny. Still searching from time to time. We don't actually collect the remains. Just sort of guide others to them. I figure you'll learn all about it later on."

This was getting weirder by the minute. The bartender had nailed it.

"We owe it to our buddies," he said again. "Can't let them be forgotten."

"Don't mean to be rude," I said, "but aren't you pretty, well, pretty senior to be on a government assignment?"

He bit off his words. "Look, Sonny. I told you this was a special detail."

I nodded. But what he was saying didn't make sense.

I needed to use the restroom. When I returned, I had plenty of questions that needed answers. But the Sergeant-Major had disappeared. And the bartender had vanished as well.

On my way to the exit, I called out. But I elicited no response.

The lights on the establishment's roof had been extinguished, and the parking lot lay smothered in wet blackness. The rain pounded down and blew sideways as I maneuvered on to the highway. I remember nothing of the remainder of my journey that night.

Seized with weariness, when I reached my hotel room, I stumbled to my bed and, fully-clothed, collapsed into an exhausted sleep. I'd barely made it. Outside, the typhoon capered across the Ryukyu Islands and slammed them hard. The wind groaned and bayed, as if in a world gone mad. It stomped on us for the better part of two days. Mostly, I slept or sat in a chair reading, waiting for the storm to pass.

Then and later, the recollection of my drive through the typhoon repeatedly traversed the landscape of my mind. As it did so, I struggled to decipher what was real and what might have been imagined. Much of what had transpired that night remained a blur and trying to recall the details carried me out of myself.

In any case, I elected not to share the story with colleagues, particularly that portion dealing with the Sergeant Major. I could imagine the raised eyebrows such a telling would elicit.

Six weeks later, I again had occasion to drive to the north end of the island on business. It turned out to be a pleasant day, with radiant sunshine and the azure skies and ocean waters of the sort the Okinawan people rightfully boasted about. On impulse, I decided to stop at Vinnie's Roadside. Warm beer and stale chips notwithstanding, the place afforded a convenient location to take a break. Moreover, despite my efforts to dismiss recollections of the earlier visit, I was curious. I wondered if I might run into the Sergeant Major, a truly strange fellow. Like a melting shadow, a satisfactory recollection of our meeting evaded me. Who was he really?

This time when I pulled in, cars packed the parking area. In the bright light of day, the place appeared less tacky than I remembered it. Apparently, Vinnie's had undergone a renovation. Fresh white paint had done wonders for the dark exterior I recalled. And, a red neon sign had replaced the feeble yellow one that guided me in the night of the typhoon.

Inside, scarfing up sandwiches and downing Budweisers, a roistering crowd of servicemen, base workers, and Okinawan girls occupied spots at the bar and at half a dozen tables. A smog of smoke fueled by Camels and Luckies filled the room. Air conditioners hummed. Country and western tunes wailed from an orange and green jukebox.

I clambered up onto a bar stool and scanned the room. No sign of the Sergeant Major.

A bartender, a big white guy in a Hawaiian shirt asked, "What's your pleasure?"

I surveyed the menu he handed me. "Looks like you've really expanded the bill of fare since I was last in," I said.

He sent me a quizzical look. "When were you here?"

"During the last typhoon. Six or seven weeks ago."

"I guess you're pulling my leg. We've only been open a couple of weeks. We sure haven't changed the bill of fare."

"Well, it was night, and..."

"You must have us mixed up with some other place. Anyway, what'll you have?" The bartender chuckled in a derisive way.

"No. This is Vinnie's. I'm sure it was here."

"Fact is this was an old wreck of a building. Closed for years. We kept the name. That's about it."

"You got another bartender?"

"Just Mr. Nagasue down there."

"Nobody else?"

"Well, when we're busy, Harvey Schmidt pitches in. He's the manager."

None of this added up. A surge of trepidation rippled through me.

"You ever have a customer people call the Sergeant Major. Old guy."

"Active duty?"

No. Probably retired."

"Not that I know of. But, like I said, we just opened."

I ordered a burger and a cold beer. But my stomach churned, and I could finish neither. What was going on?

I placed some money on the counter and got up to leave. By chance, a framed group photo behind the bar caught my eye. Eight or ten men in combat gear, lost in the black and white stream of time. A hand-lettered sign topped the faded photo: KIA. Heroes. April 1945.

"Who are those men?" I said.

"Well, Vinnie, the guy had this place after the war, had been in the battle. I guess they're some of his buddies who got killed. Found it in a backroom We hung it up. Tradition. You know."

He reached up, took the picture down, and handed it to me. "Can't imagine you'd know any of these guys. Way before your time."

"Yeah before my time." I studied the photo hard. Identifications had been penned on the back. The first man in the picture was Sergeant Major John Dotson. Killed May 3, 1945. There was no doubt. My feelings pirouetted.

"That's him."

"That's who?"

"The one I asked about. The Sergeant Major."

"No kidding. And I'm the Emperor of Japan." The bartender smirked and walked away.

He didn't believe me. Nobody would believe me. But it was him.

Lawrence F. Farrar is a former American diplomat with multiple postings in Japan, Europe, and Washington, DC. His short stories have appeared seventy-five times or so in literary magazines. His work often involves a protagonist encountering the customs and morals of a foreign society.

CEMETERY TARNATION
PHIL HEAGY

Let's whisp around a ghost-world,
unscripted, unin(hibit/habit)dead.

Polite society doesn't breathe a word down here,
and 'tis comforting to harpoon your "words to live by":
Frog-march 'em into the past tense
and heigh-ho: your readymade/form-fit/bide-a-wee epitaph!

And by the way, IS the past tense?
I would be —
tombstone-scriveners keep slathering on the third person.
Why should the living have the last word
over my corpse-custard —
"For heaven's sake," perhaps?

Rise up, o Lies 'R Us,
your son's over the boneyard.
By golly, now you'll hear and see your
"Spoon River, wider than a mile" —
Every moth-mouth a Jerry Colonna!
Alas, Lazy Chatterdead's Clover
is pulled over my eyes far too soon:
Froggie comes a-corpse'n and I must hide,
uh huh.

Phil Heagy, retired librarian, lives an exciting life in rural Pennsylvania with a retired-librarian wife and happily-illiterate doggy. When not penning his (wildly unpublished) poems, he's busy chiseling out his own epitaph.

BONES / HONEY BUN / DUMPSTER NEEDLE STICK
JON BENNETT

BONES

I only worked out
my left shoulder
but it didn't help
The right shoulder got jealous
and hurt even more
These days
everything gets stiffer
except my dick.

HONEY BUN

Remember that guy
I told you about
with the ping pong ball
sized boil on his forehead?
No? Oh right,

that poem got rejected 😦

Well, it turns out
it wasn't a boil –
it was a tumor!
I just saw him
at the liquor store
buying his dinner:

Honey Buns, Fritos, Twizzlers,
and a can labeled
Generic Cancer
because, you know,
generic is cheaper.
Since last time
the boil cum tumor
had children
they're all over his face now
I almost pointed at his food
and said,
"You are what you eat!"
but I held back
by now I think
he already knows.

DUMPSTER NEEDLE STICK

"Where's my phone?"
I looked and looked
I'd folded it in a newspaper
I'd thrown
down the shoot!
The dumpster
hadn't been emptied
in a while.
There was an aluminum tray
of putrified chicken adobo,
baby diapers,
adult diapers
and, at the bottom,
a pile of syringes

swaddled in latex gloves.
I emerged
with three needles
poking
from my soul
and a hole
in the thin layer
between tragedy
and complacence.

Jon Bennett writes and plays music in San Francisco's Tenderloin neighborhood. You can find more of his work on Pandora or Spotify, or by connecting with him at https://www.facebook.com/jon.bennett.967.

FOR ROHINGA WOMEN
CRYSTAL STONE

Poet's Note: I read about the Rohingya women in refugee camps in Bangladesh. Rahima, only 15 years old, was gang-raped in the Myanmar jungle in September. I don't want anyone to forget her story. I want everyone to remember these images, shake their heads, and repeat her, "There are many things I don't understand."

The loose tooth of childhood did not bite,
it fell into the hands of the willing, making

room for the adult to grow. The toothed trees
of the jungle did not whistle or fall—that night

the wind slowed and the methamphetamine smoke
tongued the brittle bark. Her skin, new gum

for the men who held her. "I don't know why
they bit me," she said, touched the scar on her cheek.

I imagined the teeth growing right out of the gap
in her skin, now cracked, a skeletal moon glowing

over the jungle, ready to scrape the hazy hillside,
gnaw the flesh of the captors while the trees

who sat silent by her when she screamed, still
think nothing, their bark the hollowness of ears.

Crystal's poetry has previously appeared or is forthcoming in *Eunoia Review, isacoustic*, Tuck Magazine, Writers Resist, Drunk Monkeys, Coldnoon, Poets Reading the News, Jet Fuel Review, Sigma Tau Delta Rectangle, North Central Review, Badlands Review, Green Blotter, Southword Journal Online* and *Dylan Days*. Her first book came out in December 2018 from Dawn Valley Press. It's called Knock-Off Monarch.

MEASURE / OCCLUSION / BOILERPLATE
NORA COX

[MEASURE.]

a wasp waist
a coat and tails
each day a pound of flesh wearing away
a she thinning in the cave

new soft scales, skin forming in her place

three-fourths of her flesh is held in water
one-fifth of her bone is held in water

If she burns, along with the rest, about one-twelfth of she
is left as ashes and insoluble.

lime around the thresholds

*

begin again. another call.

The shape of her body is outlined in bone.
Two hundred six bones in a normal body. Twenty-six backbones.

*

In her passage

at the ends of bones, at the ends of you and me, joints slip past
each other like plates.

*

a dried bone is two-thirds lime. soaking her in a mixture of one part
hydrochloric acid in ten parts water will remove the lime, leaving her
/ the bone so soft as to be tied, in a knot. burning her / the bone will
remove the connective tissue and leave the lime to float—in the exact
shape of the bone.

explains why she has replicas, takes shape from the ends of others.

*

carnage covers the ends of each bone, in a movable joint. a layer joins
the bones in immovable joints. the young ones are mostly carnage.
(Or, "cartilage.")

When we press on her long bones, she grows crooked and deformed.

when she grows she takes up more lime in the bones

*

to receive blood from the veins
to send blood to the interior

she bursts, she wakes.

an animal can't live in she, and she can't support "the burning in a
fire."

*

There is a point at which
what is hidden
rises and escapes
is no longer
waiting, dormant

held by what comes up through a sieve

[OCCLUSION.]

They are certain. One of them along my spine, a coiling around the ribs, head downward. At the end of the occlusion: la bête noire.

a lateral cut to extract the viscera
/ in the middle of the play stripped of bone /

she gathered the dis-membered ones
in thousands of pieces

they took their places, drifting...

[BOILERPLATE.]

we ate in the foundation
drank cemeteries

I / she can no longer bear the sound
of my / her own voice

now grown cannibalistic.

though we've grown accustomed to the taste

not all are equal

I spread my spent blood
(smeared from femoral artery)

onto my thighs

we spread the dust
into a paste

a mask of soot on her face.

my memory leaches out the bone / the memory of a hull

Nora Cox grew up in Indiana but has spent the last 10 years in Colorado, where she earned her MFA in Writing & Poetics from Naropa University. A former teacher, Nora now works at Denver Public Library as a librarian. Her poems are part of an unpublished manuscript called the book of she, which is loosely based on the volcanic eruption that took place in Martinique in 1902.

AS I LISTENED TO "GNOSSIENNE NO. 3"

JOSH PRYER

Four cord of wood, an axe,
The rain, and me –
It's a familiar scene
I still don't recognize.

The worn green rain-suit,
Leaking raindrops
Into the last warm places,
As insincere as a forehead kissed.

Each cold hand, in as much pain
Possible before the numbing,
Throbs, is the organ of
A glove full of sawdust.

Swinging axe, at first swung
With youthful vigor,
Slows with age
Into thrusts of swelling rage,

As relentless striking at the wood –
Works and Daze –
Teaches me something,
Nothing but distain.

Pausing to breathe, I ponder why
An impotent man without a virtue
Assumed a son in holy marriage,
Assumed the scepter...

Still I seek the man's approval,
Long to hear a foreign tongue.
Me and I and the rain
Rage into the night,

And the breaking of wood not unlike
The sound of thunder,
That mocking silence,
Echoes eternally in my skull

As expressions of love are dammed by lips.

Josh Pryer (07/07/1993) is an American musician and poet. Currently, he lives in Los Angeles, CA, and is earning a degree in Comparative Literature.

CHARON / BE CAREFUL WHAT YOU READ / A BONE TO PICK
E. J. HAGADORN

CHARON

He lives in death, eternal slave
To river Styx, his boat a grave.
And no reward there is for him;
No happy dance with seraphim,
Nor Hell-tormented, caught and bound,
Though many fates there are beyond.
Whilst watching sand fall in the glass,
His servitude will never pass.
And therefore he will never see
The lands of Purgatory,
Nor Paradise's azure vault,
Inferno's punishment of fault.
Straight on into Oblivion
He'll row his cargo on and on.
And if the choice were his to make
Of where his agony would slake,
I cannot guess which path he'd take,
For aught would be a welcome fix
To rowing on the river Styx.

BE CAREFUL WHAT YOU READ

One night atop the northern tower,

Where many a contemplative hour
I passed with books of lore,
I came across a dusty tome,
That far had traveled from its home,
Transcribed in days of yore.

The tales therein were of a kind
No mortal now can easy find
When law forbids them all.
So stayed I there another night,
The candle burning down its light,
With stories that enthrall.

But had I known what sort of book
I'd taken on myself to look,
I might have had it burned;
For magic was within that lore,
And Death came closer to my door
With every page I turned.

And when I put it on the shelf,
I saw an image of myself
Reflected in the glass.
One night had come and gone for me,
But while my eyes bewitched had been,
A hundred years had passed.

A BONE TO PICK

There was a dead man named Jones,
Who had rotted away to his bones.

Then the gravedigger tried
To burgle him blind,
So he kicked the old man in the stones.

E.J. Hagadorn is an author who once used an animal bone as a letter opener. His many works of fiction and poetry can be found at www.ejhagadorn.com, while his adventures in graveyards are documented at www.authorgraves.com.

THE ONLY BONES THAT SHOW
TOM LEINS

1. The hardest bone in the human body is the jawbone.

My face slams into the royal blue wall tiles at Parkside public toilets. The tiling has been polished to a deep gleam. Someone around here really takes pride in their work.

I slide down the wall and taste metallic trough-piss. At least one of my teeth comes loose and floats lazily towards the rusted drain, which is clogged with pubic hair, bloody phlegm and even a condom wrapper.

I pluck it out of the thick yellow stream and thrust it into my pocket. I haven't lost a tooth yet – not in this fucking town.

2. The tooth is the only part of the human body that cannot repair itself.

The man standing over me is called Tony 'Uncle Bones' Bonino. He is only 5'7", but his compact torso is hard like brick. I handed Marie Andretti three of his teeth in a Bastins padded envelope last week. She prefers her revenge to be carried out with a... biblical sensibility.

Bonino had hit a kid in one of her boy-brothels the previous week, and he split his head on a trunk full of sex toys, losing a couple of teeth in the process. Bones and Marie were distant cousins, but she still wanted her grisly trinkets wrenched out of his gummy smile – and she paid me to do it.

3. A pack-a-day smoker will lose approximately two teeth every ten years.

Uncle Bones slides a pack of Silk Cut out of his breast pocket and sparks up a cigarette. He exhales in my direction, and the nicotine briefly replaces the pissy stink lingering in my nostrils. He glares at me, but his eyes lack genuine hostility, and he wears his defeated look uncomfortably, like a cheap Torbay Road sports jacket.

"I get it, son. You're just the hired hand. You get me in the same room as her. I want what is mine."

I nod, and he flashes me a gap-toothed grimace, before hoisting me out of the trough, twisting my arm sharply behind my back, and marching me out of the toilet block.

I blink the fizzy piss out of my bloodshot eyes and lurch towards a silver Vauxhall Cavalier that has been double-parked on Parkside Road. I open the car boot – without being told – and climb inside.

4. Humans produce excessive saliva before vomiting to protect the teeth from the acid in the vomit.

The early evening sky above the block of flats is the colour of clotted blood. Uncle Bones lurks in the shadows as I ring the buzzer. When I yank the door open he melts through the gap like a fat ghost. I consider throwing a punch, or stomping the backs of his legs, but the rat-tail sap dangling from his clammy hand puts me off. He grabs my wrist again and contorts it behind my back.

"After you, son..."

We take the stairs rather than the lift, and Bones wheezes with effort, abandoning his half-smoked Silk Cut on the first landing.

I bang on Marie's door with the flat of my hand, and Bonino is behind me, pressed against me as intimately as a lover. We listen for her footsteps over the low thud of our mingled heartbeats. I hear the muted jangle as the security chain is unfastened, and slam my head backwards into Bonino's skull. I feel his nose shatter, smearing snot and blood across my hair, so I do it again.

When I turn around his jaw is scummed with bloody drool, and a couple of mangled teeth protrude from his ruined top lip. He scrambles back down the hallway, vomiting over his silk shirt. I unclip the blood-red fire extinguisher from the wall and drift towards him.

5. No two people have the same set of teeth – they are as unique as your fingerprint, so be proud them.

When Marie finally opens the door, she is wearing a black lace bra and panties, her elderly bones jutting out at awkward angles that remind me of a crash victim. Her complexion is crinkly like chicken skin, and her perfume gives off a damp, exotic stink.

I pass her the dripping fire extinguisher and scatter the bloody teeth across her soft beige carpet. She takes a deep lungful of smoke from one of her black-market cigarettes, and purrs.

"I don't know if I ever told you before, but you make my bosom swell with pride."

I nod. Once or twice.

Bonino's bones creak as I drag his limp body out of the hallway and into Marie's bathroom, heaving his lumpen form into the tub.

Marie passes me a drink – rum and full-fat coke. I take a sip, but my mouth still tastes of piss, and I don't enjoy it.

I don't even need to ask what will happen to Uncle Bones. Later tonight he will be dumped in a petrol-soaked squat with a handful of random junkies who are in hock to Marie. One of her coked-up second cousins will drop a match through the letterbox, and by the time their ashy bodies are raked into evidence bags in the morning they will only be identifiable by their half-rotted teeth.

Apart from Uncle Bones, that is.

His teeth will be removed with Marie's father's old chisel and stashed in her floor-safe – with the rest of her ghoulish bone-coloured baubles.

Tom Leins is a disgraced ex-film critic from Paignton, UK. His short stories have been published by the likes of Near to the Knuckle, Akashic Books, Shotgun Honey, Flash Fiction Offensive, Horror Sleaze Trash and Spelk Fiction. He has published two novelettes, Skull Meat and Snuff Racket, and two short story collections, Meat Bubbles & Other Stories (Near To The Knuckle) and Repetition Kills You (All Due Respect). https:// thingstodoindevonwhenyouredead.wordpress.com/

SHE NEVER SPEAKS
DAVID SETH SMITH

in the waning day
you hear the clinks
and scrapings
of an understanding companion
the odd friend
who carries the bones
aligned simpatico
the skull tilts
shoulder blade downturned
in a credible wince
at the sorrows, then
in the truest form
of empathy
moves inside
takes up residence
setting a lamp
that does not light
on a small table
this tableau silhouettes
against your
translucent flesh as
she casts bones
upon the table
and reads them by
pointing at the patterns
but she never speaks
she casts the bones
she never speaks

David Seth Smith Has been published in "Uncommon Minds: Autism Poetry, Prose and Short Stories" and is currently contributing editor for BlogNostics.net.

STAR IN THE SAND
DAMIAN CAMPANA

Cade walked through the red sand of the Ula'jro Desert. Each grain of sand stung as it hit his calloused torso. He looked at his staff, and a crimson glow travelled through his body. Cade, using his skeleton hand, slammed the staff between his feet sending an explosive force through the storm. The glow faded as the storm dissipated. He collapsed under his own weight and lost hold of the staff. He crawled a few feet, but only the sun and hills of red sand greeted him.

Cade raised his hands to his head. He looked back at the humanoid skull smiling atop the staff. He studied the face for the first time in years. His memory was cast back to the final battle when he claimed the staff. He remembered torrents of fire cascading from the burgundy titan's mouth burning several of his friends. He remembered the titan crushing his friends under Its feet. He remembered scaling the titan's leg using his swords. He remembered knowing he had to get the staff away from the titan. He remembered grabbing the staff with his left hand, radiance pulsing out, and feeling a searing pain as his skin and hand muscles dissolved. He remembered his world falling to darkness.

"What're you doing all the way out here, Mister?" a little voice called.

Cade blinked pulling himself back to the present. He looked around and saw a boy crest over a dune behind him. The boy wore an old potato sack held up with rope for a belt. Cade locked eyes with the boy. The boy's head tilted to the left.

"I could ask you the same thing, kid," Cade said. "Come here." The boy walked closer, taking short cautious steps. "It's dangerous to be out here alone."

"Ain't you alone too?"

Cade grinned.

"What happened to your hand?" the boy asked.

"I lost it in a battle." Cade stared at the frail boy. "What's your name?"

"Sable." The boy extended a hand.

"Cade." He shook the boy's hand and sat relieving his knees.

"Is that scary staff yours?"

Cade looked back at his staff. "Well," he sighed, "Yes, it is."

"Did it make your hand like that?"

"Yes."

"Does it hurt?"

"Not anymore." Cade trailed off clenching and unclenching his skeleton hand. His head pounded with a dull pain. "How long have you been out here, Sable?"

"I don't know. I've been walking an awfully long time."

"Sit down and rest for a bit." Sable sat down an arm's length away from Cade. The wind echoed off the dust in the otherwise empty desert. "The sun is going to roast us if we stay here too long," Cade said. "Do you want to come with me?"

"Sure."

Cade stood and grabbed the staff. "Then follow along. Let's find some shade."

The two walked in tandem and didn't speak. They continued over several hills searching for somewhere safer to rest. "Do you know why the sand is red here?" Sable asked, breaking the silence.

"No, do you?"

"My Daddy used to tell me stories about heroes and wars. He said the desert was where all the wars finally ended. He also said so much blood was spilt that it turned the sand red. He'd joke there are still people and titans buried under the sand, and that's why the color stays red."

"That's a rather gruesome story," Cade said.

"Daddy shared all sorts of stories. He knew everything like how the heroes in the final war protected the world from the titans. He always knew just what to say to make things better."

"Where's your father now?"

Sable's brow furrowed. "I...I don't know." The wind exposed an object atop one of the dunes. "Mister Cade, what's that?" Sable said.

Cade climbed the dune and poked the motionless object with the staff. A sudden ache pulsed through his head as he unburied a body.

"Oh," Sable whispered staring at the corpse.

Another wave of pain pulsed through Cade's head as he saw a deck of cards on the corpse's side. "I..." He shook his head. "Let's keep walking."

He grabbed Sable's arm and moved him away from the corpse. They continued through the Ula'jro meandering about. Cade thought back to the last time he went into the town named Thegerys. He remembered freezing outside the beaded curtain of a medium's shop. An old man had sat on a blanket. He remembered the old man's arms were covered in tattoos including a skull with three eye holes. "I sensed your presence from a mile away," the old man had said and pulled a deck of cards from behind him. "I'm called Teran. Would you like a reading?"

With Sable beside him, Cade turned around to face his staff. He threw the staff past the boy into the sand.

"Mister Cade, what's going on with you?"

Cade dropped to his knees. He glared at the staff. He again remembered Teran as the old man placed The Hanged Man, The Star and The Devil on the edge of his blanket. "You're conflicted, Cade," he had said. "You've sacrificed your willpower, yet you hope your sacrifice will end the suffering of others you care about. You fear willpower alone can't destroy whatever it is that haunts you." Cade remembered lifting the staff but stopping midstride. His eyes had rolled in the back of his head. He had turned and slammed the staff into Teran's hand. Cade remembered commanding Teran with a foreign voice to give him the cards and crawl into the desert eating sand until he became one with the sand.

"Mister Cade, what is it?"

Cade shook his head wincing. "Sable, destroy the staff."

Sable hesitated and reached for the staff.

"Wait!" Cade shouted holding out his skeleton hand.

Sable picked up the staff and immediately threw it back down. "It...it talked to me."

Cade pushed Sable away and picked up the staff. His eyes rolled back. The skull's eyes flashed, and sand wrapped around Sable's legs.

"Mister Cade! What are you doing?" The sand slithered up his torso. "Mister Cade!"

Cade watched the sand solidify around Sable. He spun around slamming the staff into the sand. He gritted his teeth and slammed the staff again, sand flying everywhere.

"No!"

The red glow of the staff faded, but he continued slamming the staff into the sand.

"No!"

Cade's tears were caked to his face. A single dark cloud appeared above him.

"No!"

Thunderbolts struck each time Cade slammed the staff. Cade stood up and kicked the skull cracking the forehead inward. The cloud faded. Cade saw red glass around him.

"Help," Sable whispered.

Cade saw scorch marks emblazoned down the left side of Sable's face. "I'm sorry." He peeled the thin sheet of glass off and eased the boy down to a sitting position. He removed his scarf and wrapped the cloth around the boy's head.

"Mister Cade?" Sable asked breaking the silence.

"Yes?"

"Are you ok?"

Cade looked at his skeletonized arm and the broken staff. He met Sable's gaze. "Sable, you saved me."

They set up a makeshift campsite in silence. Cade created a small fire using the top half of the staff. The fire poured from the skull's mouth. Cade threw the staff into the fire. Sable yawned, and Cade saw just how young the boy was when his yawn travelled through his full body.

"Mister Cade?"

"Yes?"

"It talked to you, didn't it?"

"Yes."

"My father used to say magics like that existed, but I didn't think it was true."

"Your father was right about a lot of things."

"Well I'm glad it's gone now." Sable leaned on his elbows lying down.

"I'm going to help you find your father, alright?"

Sable smiled. "Okay! Thank you. Goodnight, Mister Cade."

"Goodnight. Get some rest."

Within a few moments, Sable was snoring.

Cade unfolded the three dusty tarot cards. He ripped The Devil and The Hanged Man cards in half and tossed both into the fire. Cade crawled over to the sleeping boy. He slid The Star into his small hand and looked at the sky. He lay down and looked up at the stars. The red sand and glass was cool on Cade's skin. Cade stared at the fire and watched the staff burn.

Damian Campana is a creative writing student in New York. He is an aspiring creator. He is passionate about telling stories through different aspects of art including music, acting, writing, and drawing.

THE NECROMANCER
JAMES BURR

A lone figure bends over his work bench
Chanting some word strange to mortal men
An arm here a leg here
Soon his army will rise
The lands will run red with blood
The called him a heretic they called him mad
He will be the one to show them what true power is
His army feels no pain they fell nothing at all
They have cast off there mortal coil long ago.
He brings the bones back to life to do his will.
The army he now commands marches into the night.
Just the sound of bone scraping against stone
The necromancer's time is nigh
Fear his army of bones for it's time for you to die.

James Burr is an aspiring poet who likes to find the dark in the world and try to turn it in to beauty tough words. In his free time he enjoys playing with his ferret, and going to movies.

SILENCE
CHRISTOPER MITCHELL

in a bunker, hidden by concrete, covered by dirt, smothered
and unmoved, lies a different kind of villain. his plan
executed by maps of moss and soft stones, guided by
a single, ash grey intuition huddling around spicy embers.

what must happen before the death rattle strikes? who
will be around when the last breath comes? neither
ghosted minds nor paths blocked by marble slabs will
quit the stabbing, the throttle, the exactness, the cutting.

he will wait alone, unencumbered by friends missing
from an imagined life. his bones will gather maggots,
spiders, salamanders. his skull a great ironic island
in the unlit sand, discarded inside a moribund cube.

history will be timeless. silent.

on discovering him the sweat grows moist,
choking as if it were ectoplasm from a spirit.

i have found my perfect rival.

we are both skeletal, revamped into something
close to human. but I am here. i scrape by.

i will apprentice myself to win this game.

age old and complete. darning socks with webs

to wait out the silence.

this is all true.

Christopher Mitchell was born in Lubbock, TX, grew up in Louisville, KY, and moved to Kansas City, MO from the Northeast about 15 years ago. He is 48 with two daughters.

FOLIE A DEUX
ANNIE BLAKE
FOR MY HUSBAND, AND CHILDREN

she follows me like the children strung up during the war they teach
my children that soldiers were honorable only women are left some
tear up letters some tear up floorboards
with the hooks of hammers he told me he pulled out a fist of nails a
porcupine
i tell him that mothers would rather kill their children than not have
anything to eat fathers eventually give what they can't even if they
never die to war
*

we are not meant to save the world or live on mars he laughs for the
wheel of fortune
is fast and subliminal but crying wheels are also round and trains
don't ever run out
of steam
*

i stand between a wall and a boom gate intrapsychicity and my
interpersonal world collude step into song i play the organ's keys
with my right hand and even with my left the pedals with my feet i
wait for the train's hum the angels are singing now
they always have i'm in a trance plagued by bodies catapulted in the
middle of the next city square and biological warfare we have fixed
this cadence sealed her song anosognosia the acoustic range of the
sea is an entirely different matter we are already flying into the other
world
*

we take them to war like he wants us to i wait till the steam dresses
the sky i don't look

---

at windows actually lately i have how some tug on their collars
children tug
at their thighs i never touched my father that way he's on the train he
half knows
that soldiers are not integrated enough to deliver their promised rain
percepts
can be unconscious he knew but he just couldn't lift his eyes before
the rise of the gate i wait for the other black carriages to pass rolling
back their round wheels of tombs i hold
a string tie it around my chest cross it over for strength the calvary
cross tatzenkreuz for they walk with their feet not the swastika for
the west has blackened the cross forever diwali children the cross
pattee their feet look more like the cradle of a candelabrum
*

how they follow me across the tracks my husband tells me he loves
me i open my head
into the sky my daughter looks just like him my other daughter looks
just like his mother my son is divergent just like me
*

he lifts the stub of a rose colored candle we forgot that candles were
once alived by fire
the rain can feel as sharp as icicles i always blunt the sharp ends of
sticks to avoid injury
to the eye god's rod sticks of conversions my mother's mop hair like
medusa
my father thought that if he smacked me hard enough i would turn
into a butterfly he smacked our dog with a bat until he killed it i don't
know the real reason he didn't take him to the vet i could hear them
at the dead side of the house it wasn't really dead my mother's
impatiens grew there green and quick like the color of witch's skin
*

up the stairs in the tower he shows me candles the re-emergences of
their upward falls sometimes i only see dark mouths of the rocking
cradles of chalices the dawn rises
with its sweet yellow bread open moist mouths of starlings
threadbare skins veins like skeins
*

she comes to eat me when i'm alone and i wonder now whether i was
right to want to give her my body that way given the choice i would
rather give her the time to chew deep enough to lead them across the
show unfold peripheral and lateral vision unpin nails
to make arms as strong as wood scarf joints with keys trim their nails
even though i have often cut too far i am sorry to see the sting in
their eyes not sorry
to burn my own hands on their water faces
*

i count how they come back for me
that i can die must mean that i can live
*

as i walked with him i noticed my bag was open paper clips fall out
white pebbles
in the snow fathers who leave their children in the woods to die often
eat off their riches
even if their stepmother dies too only the father can save me now i
was young
in those days so was he the boy who promised he loved me i let things
fall out
of my arms my guilt sticking like nails into his cross
*

the ego is high-pitched notes on the treble clef the world of illusion
many people confuse illusion with allusion denotations i exhume
children from asphalt graves for connotations sometimes
psychiatrists are unable to differentiate between transference and the
meshing

of transference with countertransferential affect the unconscious the
bass clef voices
of men who can fly ego smoke curling its dust figs or figments into
clouds
like white hair from the factory the ego flashes like the siren of a
police car the corner shop opens its mouth its ejection i'm a dvd it
makes me play whatever it wants me to see
*

my mother made me a swing on a balcony she ate in a room from the
street i walk up
the stairs hold onto the balustrades brahmadanda the rising windows
of city bridges
are so beautifully fragile i tell myself i will break them if i walk across
i asked my husband if we should give our girl a wall instead of a
canvas art should never wrap nor enclose the roofs of houses are
tightly pulled in by thick sewing thread skin like corrugated iron the
church spire needles up one way to heaven
*

i have bought myself spotted black stockings the contagiousness of
chicken pox evocation of a proxy a woman keeps trying to sell me a
vintage hat with a bow it is waterproof
and everlasting like the scales of fish i walk off on her she smiles i
smile as my daddy takes photos of me while i wade into the river he
wants me to wear her hat the water
is in black and white monochrome my hat is aqua i am 25 years
younger than i really am i don't have to watch for rocks under the
surface
*

i remind myself i'm safe now that i don't have to let the memory take
me it is a memory from the past not a current event it is what i feel
when i remember i didn't understand
what i did that my mother and father would never love me again
sometimes i believe

i can go for a day trusting my inner tuition instead of years thinking i
don't understand
the hours that wake up a word the memory of my feelings roll back a
smaller wheel
*

my father never really took photos of me wading into a river and i
never really smiled
after middle school i used to just stare at things like he did i do
remember him with black hair he smiled in a video recording once
and once i saw him cry
*

my mother is cooking stew her knuckles white in her face hollow
contours
her eyes hard rounds of nails jawline like her father's her lips open
jarred and bone dark cave she always wore old woman clothes i used
to pray in a convent
because she was made to marry a man instead when i woke up and
she was gone i opened my hands and felt for the spot on her table
where the pot kept it warm
*

parietal art hand stencils communication is possible through rock
walls i shine the light on the animal painting and the shadow forms
the whole picture my ancestors
must have known that spirits come from the good and evil side of god
*

bird men heads men have beautiful arms solid curvature with the
peeking tongues
of branches how they open their beaks their translucent lids when
the rain flows
we call them flowers they pick them from the field the way he bows
his elbows
and heaves into my pits the new birds will come to eat
*

people don't need to hide behind the door they don't even have to
speak for hardly anything i see makes me laugh anymore it occurred
to me like jack out of his box
i am the wood i lay the swivels of my wrists mobility of my hips i am
blocks timber of forearms brachioradialis there is no need to convert
anything
*

city buildings erections in the sky sucking whatever water is left
cellophane windows pillars propping up the ceiling of the sky
windows decks of cards shuffled and worn out by players winter is the
time of the yellow lights in the city they hang like stars
my ancestors hang them from their arms out of their fingertips
starlings so i can drive forward into the road like a spade shoveling
snow their safe hand is what i owe
the creases in palms fingers old river and sanctuary roads
*

i unpack my bag in hospital a photo of my child the sanction of my
wings on her back
and her smile
*

to remind me why i need to come home

Annie Blake is an Australian writer and divergent thinker. She is a wife and mother of five children. She started school as an EAL student and was raised and, continues to live in a multicultural and industrial location in the West of Melbourne. Her research aims to exfoliate branches of psychoanalysis and metaphysics. She is currently focusing on in medias res and arthouse writing. She enjoys exploring symbology and the surreal and phantasmagorical nature of dreams. She is a member of the C G Jung Society of Melbourne and Existentialist Society in Melbourne. You can visit her on annieblakethegatherer.blogspot.com.au and https://www.facebook.com/profile.php?id=100009445206990.

THE CLOSER THE BONE...
DIANE ROOT

The tombstone on his property, barely blurred by the passage of time or weather, stood alone in the woods, where he claimed his first wife liked to walk. It read: Matakia Rose Albinelli. She died at 33.

Mysteriously.

She was weak of heart, her husband said, but nothing that would have made him anticipate a sudden death like this. He was out of the country at the time, and for that reason, he couldn't for the life of him surmise even the remotest possibility of her demise.

Had anyone investigated, which, of course, they did not, they would have found him with the turquoise-eyed blonde beauty, appropriately named Marie as befitting her appearance. He had encountered her on a beach in Nice on the Riviera. She looked great in a bikini. She looked even better without one.

He found that the sun-streaked, pastel city of Nice—a place that seemed to predominantly favor a blinding white, a faded rose and an unlikely shade of mustard for its buildings–was a great place to be nice. And Marie was nice. Very nice, very Nice. This, he decided, was not destined to be just some run-of-the-mill summer romance. No, this was an amatory addiction with a capital A. Two of them, in fact.

He resolved right then and there to bring her back to the United States and set her up in a cozy place of her own, close by. Already devoted, she did not hesitate. Her own home town, coincidentally also Marseille like his wife's birthplace, was a tiny pied a terre on the fringes of the great maritime, often murderous city would doubtless prove to be a hovel next to what awaited her abroad. It was a decision easily made—not unlike the maid herself.

Apart from that, such was their passion that "pensees" turned to "poison " way before then. Digitalis seemed like a good idea.

"What fun," he said. "It's like a finger pointing to the about-to-perish. Digitalis and Drambuie, drop by drop in every evening's digestif. What could be a better match?" Digitalis. Digital. (He didn't say which digit.) What he did say was "Delightful!" With nothing short of glee.

***

Indeed, she could not have been more unlike her predecessor, who was a young, voluptuous woman, curvaceous, full-breasted, and olive-skinned with a mane of ebony hair and melted-chocolate eyes. Wife #1 was a Mediterranean beauty. Very Mediterranean—born in Marseilles of Greek-Italian origin and a trace of Turkish—she harbored old-school beliefs, which he had found endearing.

She believed, for instance, in the Evil Eye, a talisman that dangled from her wrist on a charm bracelet among various other souvenirs of their travels together and many he brought home when he traveled alone.

But The Eye, the one of which she was most fond, was a gift from her mother, the formidable Jeanne Rose despite her small stature. Maman instructed her to wear it always without fail. "Meme au lit," she said. Then after a short pause, she added, "Surtout au lit." ("Even in bed—above all in bed.") Even her daughter's name, Matakia, was a diminutive of mati , meaning "eye" in Greek.

Rooted in ancient civilizations as diverse as Mesopotamia, Egypt, Phoenicia, Greece (there are even mentions in the Old Testament), the belief in the evil eye seemed deeply ingrained. It held that a scourge could be released from the mere malign glance of its believers, no matter their age. No matter how often denied, the deeply-held superstition ran submerged through their veins like blood. The gaze could curse, not only the one beheld, but their mate, their offspring, as well as future generations and property. Present and future could be afflicted with misfortune, illness, death and drought, plague and pestilence.

Her rival, Marie, was everything she was not.

Matakia's amulet, alas, did not save her. Nor did her name. They did something infinitely worse.

***

Soon Marie was a frequent guest for dinner; the host/ husband encouraged, ever gracious not to mention generous, the friendship between the two women. He arranged "surprise" outings for them—the theater, museums, concerts, shopping trips, and whatever else he could conjure up, especially when he was not in the city. "You need a companion," he said by way of explanation to his wife who was by nature of a rather solitary bent—unusual for someone of her origins.

But then again, she was a writer, and that in his mind explained everything should anyone had asked. Thankfully, nobody did. Despite all his deviously soothing endeavors, the silences between them grew longer and longer. "What, my darling, is the matter?" he would ask, feigning a plaintive voice, both saccharine and solicitous.

She would just stare him down, the chocolate eyes flashing ebony, blackening in a dark fury. And deeply suspicious. It was the same ebony glare she turned upon Marie at the end of their last supper. But this time, she spoke in a low growl, "You will be the most accursed among women." Rigidly erect, she turned away leaving the lovers slack-jawed and, for once, robbed of their usual banter. Marie, suddenly chilled as if by an invisible icy sheet of sleet and fractured by fear, fled.

***

Matakia soon began to feel the effects of their ministrations that ebbed and flowed within her, albeit slowly. An only child of a

153

deeply superstitious family, she knew instinctively when the golden-locked Marie, her husband's new-found "friend," came to dinner that disaster would be served up for dessert. What she didn't know, at least not immediately, was that the dessert was death.

Hers.

***

After a "decent" interval, Marie became Wife #2.

Then, not long after "an indecent" interval, as her new husband liked to jest, Marie was pronounced pregnant. By now becalmed, she settled down to become the present wife and future mother, confident that she would be courageous, in full command and control of the event.

Her "time" as they called it, wouldn't take long now.

When the Time did come, it came suddenly. The child, already named Samantha, was born without prior warning of which Marie was aware while she was in the shower early in the day. Despite the pain, she was sure that the agony would not last long. After all, she had taken care not to balloon during her pregnancy, eating carefully and sparingly for someone often incited to "eat for two."

She herself had come into the world at 11 pounds after a 48-hour agonizing parturition that doubtlessly, via guilt and shame, led her to abhor all beings rotund—most particularly human beings. Porkers, she thought. Pigs. She was convinced that bouncing babies should only bounce in moderation. This was aided and abetted by the latest new-fangled theory she had read. Thin was in. Fine by her.

***

The harrowing pains carved and shrieked, coursing and streaking through the marrow of her bones, sharp as knives. She stretched to a near-breaking point, as though torn apart on the

Inquisition's rack, rending the very fabric of her Catholic soul. Her face, at last heavenward, her archangel lips imploring for mercy, her hands gripped the metal faucets with what little strength remained. The flames of hellfire flared within her abdomen and below, searing a fiery path for this fruit of her loins, burning a passage.

Ashen, she sank to her knees.

Only then, quite some time after the scrape and scream of childbirth, the hollowing out of the beloved body from between the haunches, did she hear the clatter on the tiles and looked down.

Of the "flesh and blood" so desired and long anticipated, there was much blood and not an ounce of flesh.

Not one.

***

Post Scriptum and Post Mortem: She, too, soon lay buried beneath the bleached ivory tombstone in the woods. It was not until years later, the secret was finally unearthed, several feet beneath her and the body of the bereaved husband, revealing a small package of bones unceremoniously wrapped in a towel, by then shredded and disintegrating.

Diane Root, a dual-national, was born in Paris of an American father, the journalist and writer, Waverley Root, and a French mother. Primarily known as a painter, she is, as she describes herself, "an accidental writer." She never sought to be published but that notwithstanding, she was nonetheless published in the New York Times Magazine ("The Artful Dodger" about lunch with Picasso) and various other venues. View her art: http://matakia.com.

THE HUNTED
DAKOTA GORDON

His breath came in out in puffs; rasps of fog that drifted up, clouding his vision. It was cold, near freezing, which prompted the hunter to wonder what he was doing in the Wenaha uplands when he could be at home next to a fire drinking a warm glass of Pendleton. Ice crystals formed in his long, black hair from his exertion; sweat trickled down his neck and chilled in the air and, clinging to his locks before dripping to the forest floor. Hunting wasn't always sunshine and blood. Darkness was creeping into the forest, and needleless tamarack trees made the landscape feel barren.

In October, the Wenaha was riddled with harvest colors: oranges, reds, yellows, and greens. Now in late November, the weather was dark; whites, greys, and blacks kept the forest cast in shade. His dark green pants were drenched from the continuous sleet of rain, his wool hoodie, undershirt, socks, boots, and beanie, all equally soaked, dampening his mood as well. Despite the dampness, it was one of those moments that Wade felt truly connected to the forest.

The wood stock of his rifle was slightly warmer then the cold steel of the barrel, but his numbed gloveless hands were too frozen to feel the difference. He traded the rifle back and forth between the frozen digits, one grasping the wood while the other was pocketed for warmth. Wade knew time was against him. He was prepared for a day hunt, but an overnight adventure in the Wenaha amidst a forecasted November snow storm was more than he'd bargained for. The rain was shifting to beautiful, perilous snow-flakes in front of him.

Wade was part Algonquian; his grandmother was full-blooded Cree. Although the Wenaha was Nez Perce country, it still felt good to be in the wild. Elk and deer were plentiful in Eastern Oregon's back country. Wade had never seen the Boreal Forest of his ancestors; his grandmother had grown up there, but she had left when she was young. Wade knew the game there was dwindling; centuries of excessive fur trapping pushed by the Hudson Bay and Northwest companies had rocked ancestral hunting stock. Now development had pushed back the fringes of the boreal to the precipice of extinction. Logging, oil, and urban expansion increased pressure on the forest. Dams went up, changing ecosystems that had supported Cree for millennia. Caribou, moose, and other big game were scarce, which had prompted his grandmother's exodus. That and a young, hairy Irishmen with a timid smile. Wade missed his grandfather, who had spent most of his youth chasing his grandmother through the Boreal. He hoped to see it while there was still something wild to see.

Get back to the truck, the thought brought Wade back to his present predicament. He needed to make it back to the mountain road where his truck was parked, and he'd be alright. The sleet was quickly turning to snow as the temperature dropped, propelling him faster through the gloom as white stuck to the forest floor. The light was fading when he reached the edge of the meadow. Hope, he thought. That was a good name for the meadow. The salvation of a muddy pickup awaited his return on the other side of the football-field-sized clearing. He could just make out the outline of the snow-covered gas truck through the fresh falling snow. Wade felt lighter with each step as he left the darkness behind.

A slight decline from the forest edge to the meadow was separated by a running stream of water that was nearly frozen for the winter. Wade was steaming from the exertion of the hard push back to the truck; hot blood ran in his family. He recalled his grandfather walking through the snow during elk season with his wool shirt and jacket unbuttoned. His family would stand huddled around a campfire, as they always did at elk camp. They chatted and chattered, shivering from the cold as the snow fell around them. His grandfather would come trudging up to them with his wool undershirt unbuttoned to his waist, his grey chest hairs and naked belly defying the weather, and hot steam would broil outwards like fog. His grandmother would shake her head and mutter something about hot blood that drew a smirk from the old man. Wade smiled at the memory and commemorated it by loosening the drawstring on his own wool shirt. Everything but his fingers had thawed from the fast pace. Although warming, the pace had worn Wade out. He wasn't thinking of the best route to his pickup, only the most direct. It was unusual for Wade to be out hunting alone, especially so close to dark. He always hunted with family or close friends, but the nearness of Thanksgiving and his family's tradition of eating deer to celebrate the holiday had compelled him to venture alone, and this year his family needed the deer to make it through the winter.

Wade had found a dead tree to walk across that morning, but with the dwindling light he chose instead to slosh through the calf-deep water, careful to keep his rifle from dipping too low. The nipple and hammer stayed tucked under his left armpit to keep the cap and powder dry, and the barrel was always held slightly downward so no water could trickle in that way either. Wet powder was worthless. His older brother had taught him to carry his gun that way. Muzzle-loader hunting wasn't the easiest way to hunt, but it was a family tradition. It was also the only season Wade had drawn a tag for. Wenaha was tough to draw, but he was still in Union County where the tag was legal. Wade found he enjoyed the challenge. Hunting was the best way to put good, clean meat on the table that his family couldn't otherwise afford.

The cold water livened Wade's senses as it splashed from his calves to his knees. He didn't grimace but smiled tightly as he forged onward, remembering the time he and his older brother had crossed the Grande Ronde in a similar fashion. During the same deer season a few years prior, Wade had killed a buck in the Starkey unit. Wade and his brother each had a gun held high in one hand and an antler in the other as they had dashed across the river to the warmth of their waiting rig. That time the river had been iced over, so when they burst through the crust, the water had been unexpected. It had elicited yips of curse-filled laughter. Similar to Wade's current predicament, they had navigated the calf-deep water with haste. The cold dash had been more rewarding with a dead deer in tow. Wade made the other side of the creek and climbed up the bank to the meadow. The transition from soaking to soggy was complete. Almost home.

The deer in front of him jarred the hunter into focus. He forgot about the weather. His sopping feet didn't matter, his frozen fingers, the weight of his pack. The arthritic-like clench of his hand on the gun's underbelly eased open and his focus tunneled. All he saw was the deer. Wade slowly went into a crouch, bearing his rifle upward as he knelt and easing the hammer back to the halfcocked position. He slid the copper cap over the nipple. The cap would ignite sparks when the hammer struck it, setting the powder on fire and exploding the round ball down the barrel's rifling toward his target. The primitive nature of the weapon didn't matter. With the nearness of the deer, Wade eased the hammer back from half to full-cocked. The rifle had two triggers, the front making the back a hair trigger. He slid that back, too. The deer never noticed him, its nose pointed down, feeding. Its neck was swollen from the rut. Hormones had taken hold. Like Wade, the deer had only one thing on its mind. Wade watched it graze as snow fell around it, accumulating on its antlers. The buck was replenishing for the night, readying itself for further deer-frolicking.

Wade slowed his breathing. Despite his being a seasoned hunter, the anxiety of a buck would overtake him if he let it. Don't get buck fever. Get nervous after. That's what his dad had taught him. His dad had a million sayings, but that one always stuck. Hunters made mistakes when they got anxious. He could miss, or worse the animal could get wounded. Poor shots often meant animals ran off only to die elsewhere. Despite the ever-present carrion creatures of the forest, much of the meat would go wasted, and that he could not abide. His grandmother said wasted meet was bad luck on a hunter's family.

This year they especially needed the good luck and the sustenance the deer would provide. Good hunters always ate and utilized everything on an animal. Staying calm allowed him to abide by those laws and celebrate a clean kill. Get nervous after. He paused with his breath half exhaled. The buck lifted its head and looked right at him. Was it squinting? He didn't know if deer could squint, but he did see the opening of its throat. A white diamond-patch of hair was laid bare like the bullseye on a target. Wade gently squeezed the trigger.

Shhh-Boom!

The rifle sounded off with the typical muzzle-loader sizzle that black-powder guns make, a distinct two-part sound; first came the percussion cap and light sizzle of powder that was followed quickly by the boom of the shot. White smoke billowed out in front of him, obscuring his vision, and sulfurous burnt powder filled the air with the smell of rotten eggs. The smoke cleared. Wade could see the buck kicking its legs rapidly, flailing on the ground in the accumulating snow and churning a deer-angel into the flakes.

Wade pumped his fist into the air as he walked forward, excited for the kill. It was a large-bodied deer which meant plenty of meat. The antlers were just a bonus, bragging rights over his brother. The deer rolled over, still kicking but not rising. Wade continued his stroll toward the buck reaching for his black powder pistol, a miniature version of his rifle that he kept holstered on his right hip. To his astonishment, the deer rolled over a third time, legs kicking, and found its footing. It bounded away faster than he could draw and fire.

The ecstatic emotion of a long, hard hunt capped off with a kill quickly turned to shock and disbelief. For a buck to weather a shot from a .50 calipered rifle and get up, let alone run away, was unfathomable. Wade shook his head at the deer's audacity. He walked to the area of the shot and looked for blood but found none. No blood? He looked for an hour in the mounding snow to no avail. The adrenaline had passed, and Wade's slow, steady search for blood had yielded nothing but the bitter cold of winter. The batteries in his flashlight were dwindling and Wade knew he shouldn't risk getting lost or stuck in the blizzard. There was also the matter of the creek, which he was unwilling to cross again in the dark in order to pursue the deer. Despite the gut-turning nausea that he felt at having only wounded the deer, Wade was confident that he could find it the next day.

He crossed the meadow and headed for his rig. His flashlight was dying when Wade noticed a set of tracks by the truck. At first, he thought it was the deer, but Wade quickly realized that they were far too large for the buck. The prints were about the same width as his boots, but a few inches longer. Curling claws tucked into the snow. He didn't know what to make of it. His first instinct was bear, but the tracks were too big. There was something else that was off, something that nagged at the back of his mind. He noticed a smudge on his truck where it had brushed against the bedrail in the snow, leaving a wet streak that had yet to cover again with snow. Wade looked around, cold flakes clinging to his face. He knew it was fresh. The tracks were on top of fresh snow and had yet to fill in. It could be close enough to be watching him. His neck hairs slowly pricked up, and Wade was sure that he was being watched. He jumped in the truck and threw his gear into the passenger seat. With the heater blaring and wipers buzzing, Wade began the long descent off the mountain, pushing the strange track from his mind as his nerves settled.

Wade made it home. The descent into the Grande Ronde Valley was always beautiful at night; lights like beacons illuminated the valley floor. His family was still up, drinking in the living room and listening to music around the fire. His brother greeted him at the door.

"Any luck?"

Wade nodded as he stripped to his underwear and hung all of his gear around the hearth to dry. Wade stretched, letting his lean frame warm by the fire. He was stronger than his narrowness let on. He rubbed his shoulders where the straps from his pack had pulled down, easing out some of the tension. Light from the flames danced on his bare chest as he collected himself. His older brother bore a resemblance but with a shorter, slightly squatter frame. They had the same skin though, and the same dark eyes. Wade aspired to be like his brother, a family man who managed to stay connected with his heritage, finding success in the traditional and contemporary worlds alike.

He poured himself that glass of Pendleton and gathered some dry clothes. His brother's family included a wife, daughter, and son. Wade's grandmother also stayed at the house. The kids were in grade school, and Wade was endeared to them as only family can be. Despite the tough times, his brother had taken him in. His brother was a real estate agent who flipped houses on the side, but it had been a rough couple of years, and they'd barely gotten by. Wade had finished school at Eastern Oregon University in La Grande but had been unable to secure a job. His brother, despite having mouths to feed, hadn't hesitated in taking him in. Their grandmother had taught them to stick together. His brother never lorded it over him, but still Wade felt as though he owed them. With an empty freezer, he felt like providing a deer was how he'd pull his own weight.

Wade sat down on the hardwood floor close to the fire and stared into the flames. He let the heat warm his bones and the whisky warm his spirit. A slight smile of disbelief etched onto his cheeks as he recalled the deer's escape. He could imagine telling his grandfather about it and hearing him laugh in return. Like the deer, his grandpa had been a tough old goat, but he'd passed several winters back.

His grandmother came back from reading the children stories and sat next to him by the fire. He recounted his day to both her and his brother. She looked like something out of a history book; her long raven hair had turned grey when his grandfather died, and her face had weathered. Still, there was something comfortable about her. Her wrinkles were pleasant, like a ratty old shirt that was too important to ever discard. He got to the part about the track, struggling with telling them about it. How could he describe it in a manner that was believable? He told them anyway.

His brother squinted at him. It reminded Wade of the deer, and he made up his mind that deer could indeed squint. His grandmother looked down at her own glass of Pendleton, another quality he loved about her, and was quiet. Wade could tell she was going to talk but was searching for the right words. His sister-in-law came in and killed the music, which meant the children were asleep, and then sat with his brother on the couch. His grandmother spoke while his brother stoked the fire. Words like gravel came out in a slow, steady timbre. Wade listened intently, drinking her words like he drank his whiskey.

"Be careful when you go back for the deer." Even her voice had the comfortable sound of wrinkles. They needed the meat, he knew that, but there was something else in her tone, a crack in her voice that wavered unsteadily like the draft from a fire just before it ignites. Wade knew she wasn't just talking about the weather. "My oldest son went missing in that country when you were young."

Wade barely remembered he wasn't yet five when Uncle Joe had gone missing. That, too, was in the Wenaha, in the fall during bow season. An unexpected snow storm had hit, and Uncle Joe never made it off the mountain. All they'd ever found was his missing clothes, bare-footed tracks, and bear tracks like the ones Wade had described. The rescue team had chalked it up to hypothermia and bear scavenging and had given up on the search. Wade always got the impression that his grandmother thought it was something else.

Wade listened as she told him she'd heard stories when she was a small girl, Cree tales about the Spirit of Winter, about windigos, about famine and people resorting to cannibalism. She told him to be cautious. She averted her eyes, and Wade could tell she was holding something back, something personal that she pushed from her mind. It didn't matter, he couldn't leave the deer. It was his responsibility, not just to his family, but to the deer as well. Wade was possessive about his kill.

"It is good that you are going back for the deer." She paused and slurped some more of her whiskey. "Our people played a part in the destruction of our homeland. We sought furs as avidly as the white man, we hunted and trapped our food to the brink of extinction, until we, like that which we hunted, were in danger of losing our way of life."

Wade didn't think it was a coincidence that his own family was in a similar, albeit less dire situation. The Algonquian peoples who persevered had found a way to survive, but the plight of the Boreal continued.

"It is important that you hunt and provide for your family, but it is just as important that you do not over-hunt or kill wantonly."

Wade nodded, "I know, Grandma. That's why I am going back."

It was late when his grandmother finished her stories, his family retired to their rooms. Wade set his phone alarm for four in the morning, stoked the fire, grabbed a blanket, and lied down on the floor by the flames. His brother had to work the next day, so Wade knew he'd again be in the forest alone. Thoughts of the buck and the strange track slowly eased as Wade drifted into slumber. He stirred when his grandmother came out after midnight. The fire had died down. She pulled the blanket up around his neck, and Wade dozed back to sleep.

Four came early. Wade's tired body did not want to rise, the exertion from the hunt made him feel sorer than his age. At least it's warm. He rose slowly and rubbed his face. The lamp on the other couch flicked on, and Wade started at the sight of his grandmother. She smiled at him.

"Good morning Grandma, why are you up." Wade was still rubbing his eyes as he read four on the clock. He rose and started gathering his gear. The fresh pot of coffee and fried eggs on the counter let him know that she'd been up for a while.

"I couldn't sleep."

Wade smiled. "Did I snore?"

"Like a bear."

Wade smiled some more. He stretched, lounging outward and arching his abdomen until it elicited a slight grunt that made her laugh. His grandmother's hair was frizzled, but it still hung down to her waist. She wore a thick flannel robe which was drawn tight around her slender frame. Fiery. That was the way his grandfather had described her, and Wade found that to be an apt description. He watched as an old woman pushing eighty years of age cooed over him at four in the morning. She hugged him as he walked toward the door. He noticed a satchel by the entryway that he didn't recognize. She pulled a tomahawk and obsidian knife out of the bag and clipped it around his waist. "These belonged to my father."

Wade admired the weapons. The knife hilt was cut from an old shed horn the knotted antler made an excellent grip. Twined horse hair wrapped around the chunk of black obsidian at the base where it was set into the hilt. Wade tested the edge; it was sharper than his shaving razor. The tomahawk was equally beautiful.

She hung a necklace with a pendant carved from the base of a deer antler around his neck, "this is for protection," she said as she hugged him.

Wearing much of the same attire as he had the day before, but with fresh, dry under-wool, he headed back into the mountains feeling renewed. Wade drove, thoughts of his buck pushing the pedal down. The amount of snow on the way up the mountain was disconcerting. He figured it at just shy of two feet. He shook his head as he drove, foot down all the way to the floor, truck geared into 4-Hi, and traction control turned off so that he wouldn't bog down. Snow flew behind his tires as he pegged up the mountain. Wade's were the first tracks headed up so he didn't worry about other rigs, only getting back to the meadow to find his deer.

Day broke as Wade made the clearing. To his satisfaction, the sun seemed to part the clouds. The storm was breaking, and Wade hoped he wouldn't have to deal with any new weather fronts for a while. He parked the truck, grabbed his gear, and started tromping through the snow-filled meadow. He found the spot where the buck had taken the blast, it was fairly burrowed out still where it had writhed in the snow. No blood. Wade could see that clear as day. Wade also knew that the warmth of it would seep up through the snow with a reddish tint.

Wade was able to track the deer prints through the snow to the edge of the creek. They had filled in with snow, but they were still visible. He found the tree he'd crossed the day before. Like everything else on the mountain, it was doused in snow. Wade crossed it carefully and made his way to the other bank. He walked the edge of the creek until he picked up the deer's tracks. The tracks headed back into the forest that Wade escaped the evening before. Tree-limbs bore the brunt of the snow fall. The snow-laden canopy protected the forest floor and made it easier for Wade track the deer, whose prints were less filled in under the canopy.

Wade smiled as he squeezed through the underbrush. The only downsides to the canopy were the occasional clumps that made their way down his neck and the drifts around the tamaracks where the canopy was non-existent. He tracked the deer easily. Wade could see skids where it fell and struggled to push itself up. Despite the lack of blood, he was encouraged by this because it meant the deer had probably died wherever it curled up for the night. He figured that his lead ball had hit just below the throat and smacked into the deer's brisket, most likely flattening the ball into a pancake and breaking the deer's chest. The bone would have stopped the ball and kept the deer from bleeding externally, but it would still have bled out on the inside.

Wade trudged through another mile of snow and began to find more skids from the deer. Its struggle to regain footing was becoming clearer, its tracks fresher, and Wade grew giddy with anticipation. He knew he was getting closer to finding the buck and beginning the process of field dressing the animal and packing it back to the truck.

A dull reddish spot out in front of him let him know he was really getting close. Blood. Wade smiled as he saw a trail of red in stark contrast to its white backdrop. It disappeared under the snow-laden branches of a fir tree. He expected to find the deer dead at its base.

There was a large splash of red. Wade could see where the buck's rack had lain in the snow, the blood next to the antler marks having poured from its mouth. This is where he died. Wade was certain. The curling claws of a track next to the blood brought back the anxiety from the previous night. In his excitement over tracking the deer, Wade had pushed the bizarre prints aside. He could see where the deer had been dragged out from under the branches on the other side of the tree. Two more prints were in the snow. Long and straight, claws entrenched in the snow, dangling deep as if grabbing at the ground beneath. The hair on Wade's neck pricked up as he began following the new trail.

Wade couldn't track the bear. It must have been walking backwards and pulling the deer over its prints, obscuring them. His heart quickened as he followed the skid trail from the deer. It reminded him of kids pulling sleds behind them before they raced down a hill. The thought of confronting a bear was less intimidating with his rifle and pistol at hand but still nerve-racking, considering the primitive nature of the guns. His mind whirled along with his beating chest, trying to make some sense of it. A bear could carry food in its mouth, he knew that. He'd seen a black bear pick up a dead cow elk and walk several hundred yards with it. He'd been awestruck. He knew a deer would be no problem, but the buck had been dragged for some distance.

As he continued on, it dawned on Wade that it didn't make any sense. The blood in the trail was increasing. Wade began finding tufts of long white hair from the deer's stomach. Tufts, then blood, and then entrails. Wade shook his head in disgust as he came across the guts of the deer as they were strewn out along the snow. It was bizarre that he couldn't see where the bear had stopped to rip the deer open. The drag marks continued, and he couldn't figure out how the guts had spewed forth.

Wade stopped in his tracks as he found a chunk of lung. The brighter red of lung blood made it easy to distinguish from other organs. Anyone who'd spent much time hunting or butchering knew the color. Wade stared at the lung. A bite was missing. He realized what was bothering him so much. It was the shape. To his horror the bite mark was distinctively not bear-like. Bears had long maws and canines, but this looked like Wade could have done it himself. A short, half-moon bite was the only piece missing.

Wade realized what had been bothering him about the tracks. They were straight. Wade had come across dozens of bear tracks in the woods, and every one of them had their heels out and claws pointed in, pigeon-toed. His dad had showed him when he was little, and every bear he'd ever seen walked with its feet turned in like that. Wade went down to his knees in the snow and tried to keep calm as he scanned for a track that wasn't obscured from the carcass's drag marks. He was getting nervous, sweating with clammy anxiety instead of physical exertion.

Wade continued on the trail and kept finding half-eaten chunks of deer innards along the way. The dragging continued without pause, even where Wade found gnawed lumps of guts. He knew that whatever was eating the deer was eating while it walked. It was pulling the insides out of the deer, walking, and eating in stride.

The hunter's stomach churned with the realization. He found a chunk of tenderloin from the deer's underbelly, and he knew that he was right. Tenderloin could only be cut out after an animal was gutted. This thing was walking backwards through the snow, pulling the deer with one limb and ripping out slices with the other. He kept following the trail, terrified, but cold fascination and necessity kept his legs propelling forward. His limbs felt weighted, one lifting after the other in lifeless repetition. He remembered his dad's saying. Get nervous after. He could almost see his old man standing there, urging him to push forward. Don't kill anything you aren't going to eat. It was Wade's deer. He'd killed it to feed his family, not some forest creature. Perhaps the most compelling piece of motivation was the absurdity.

The hair and blood slowly began to trickle to a stop. Wade knew he was getting close. The ups and downs of the ridge fingers were coming together and beginning to steepen, and he could just start to see the edge of a rocky bluff in the outline through the trees. The deer-skids were heading straight for a deep, seeping hole at the base of the bluff. The mossy cave entrance made him feel sick again.

Wade was no longer tracking the blood trail from the deer there was no need. The cave entrance beckoned him, and he knew that whatever had pulled his deer through the forest had gone into its dark depths. A draft of cold air billowed out as he got closer to the entrance, buffeting him. He glanced up at the sun and realized he only had half a day left. The hunter drew his jacket tighter about him and made his way carefully across the rocks; the snow and slick sheen of blood made his footing tenuous. Wade crept toward the entrance, his heart pounding and mind racing with every step. His body stiffened and slowed in a spasm, no longer willing to do his own bidding. Wade grabbed the necklace his grandmother had given him, clutching it like an amulet, and gritted his teeth until his breathing slowed.

The slowing sensation drifted away as Wade made for the entrance of the cave. He dug into the side pouch of his pack until he retrieved his flashlight. The light seemed to chase the darkness at the edges of the cave deeper. Wade froze. For a moment he thought he could see red eyes glowing at the edges of the light. As he peered closer, he realized there was nothing there except red dots on the cave's back wall. His racing heart never slowed as he crept. Wade wished he had brought something more than his powder guns for protection.

The breeze coming out of the cave led Wade to believe that it must be deep. The smell was rank. A hint of rotting, spoiled meat filled the air, but there was something else as well, something nebulous. It reminded Wade of the strange smell of dead cougar, the stink their claws got after tearing into flesh for too long, the rancid feline odor of carnivorous eating. His family had eaten mountain cats before. Unlike deer, which only had to hang for a couple of days, mountain lions had to hang for a full week before that horrid odor would go away. As he flashed his light around, Wade realized that the cave was really more of an alcove. Native drawings lined the walls in reds and blues everywhere he turned. There was a story here, a warning.

Despite his dire situation, the cave drawings brought a moments' respite to Wade as he scanned the artwork. He could see pictographs in chalk of game dying, forests getting pilfered and the native peoples going hungry. It reminded him of his grandmother's stories from the night before. Game was being taken wantonly, and there was famine. Wade followed the pictographs with his light until he came across something that could only be described as cannibalism. Pictures etched in yellow chalk showed someone going hungry, getting lost in the forest, then murdering and eating somebody else. Then there was something else, but Wade couldn't make it out. A claw had dug into the cave wall, smearing out whatever had been drawn there. He shuddered. The rend in the wall had cut the very stone, gouging into the cave's exterior and desecrating whatever dark image lay beneath.

The flashlight caught something white and dull on one of the back walls. A bone. Wade realized there were many bones scattered across the wall. The hunter moved closer to inspect, and he could see that there was a slope on that portion of the wall. It led up to a ledge and deeper into the cave. More bones gleamed off the light. Bleached whites and sickly yellows merged in a deathly mosaic. There were old pieces of hair and sinew that had caught on the niches of the cave wall as animals had been pulled upward. There was also fresh hair, long and white, from the underbelly of a white-tailed deer. It was sticky with wet blood. Wade imagined the strength it would take to pull up a deer like that and shook his head in fearful awe. He turned back for the entrance, but the image of his grandmother shaking her head made him stop. Wade closed his eyes and grabbed his necklace again. He had to keep going. He wanted his grandmother to be proud, he didn't want his brother's kids go hungry, and he wanted to live up to his own ancestral expectations. More than that, he needed to know.

The ledge was only about ten feet above Wade's head. The hairs on his arms began to prick up. There was something else bothering him about this lair of the cave. The draft was stronger and the rank had intensified. Wade new the buck he'd shot the night before hadn't gone bad, not in the snow and cold weather, so there had to be some other dead animal emitting the stench. Once again Wade tightened his jacket and laced down his pack. He slung his powder rifle over his left shoulder and loosened his pistol in its holster. The hunter stuck the flashlight in his mouth and started up, carefully finding finger holds where he could. He had to dislodge the bones of whatever had snagged previously. As he climbed, Wade sent the pieces crashing down to the cave floor behind him. He cringed with each clank. The slight reverberations fell like an earthquake on his ears, Wade gritted through the clamor and continued. It was the only way he could climb up with all his gear.

He made the ledge and pulled himself to the top. The floor was sharp and cold, and his fingers were white with exertion. The horror of the top level of the cave came crashing down on Wade like a thunderclap. Bones were strewn everywhere. Some had been there for years, some for months, and some for less. Elk and deer antlers lined both sides of the tunnel-like chamber floors, which lead deeper into the mountain. Maws from deceased cougars, bears, wolves and coyotes were strewn about, the carcasses of predator and prey alike on display. There were two passages that went deeper, the one on his right nothing but a black hole. Wade's flashlight failed to penetrate its depths. He went down the other passage, following the droplets of smeared blood where the deer had been taken.

Wade made step by slow step down the narrowing passage, keeping his eyes off the disheartening carnage of the floor, trying to avoid the bone-lair. Eyes forward. This became impossible as Wade came across a seated, upright skeleton. He tried to look away, but the overbearing, morbid nature of the place wouldn't let him. He bent down and inspected the dead man with his light. His mind raced. Uncle Joe? It was impossible to tell, but he wondered. Wade felt another emotion bubbling in his core and mixing with his terror. Anger. He realized that some of the bones from earlier had to be human.

The light from the cave entrance was getting far enough behind that it was dark on both sides of the hunter. He flashed his light both ways, nervously checking to make sure that nothing had snuck in behind him. Wade pressed forward, leaving the skeletal remains behind. The next body that Wade came across was responsible for the smell. Maggots writhed across another dead man's face. An open wound on the side of the stomach wormed with carrion bugs. He remembered something about a hiker who had gone missing in the fall on the other side of the Wenaha. A shiver rippled up his spine. The gaping hole was somewhere near the liver, and he realized that whatever had done this had ripped the organ out whole. Like a monstrous Jeremiah Johnson, it ate the livers of its enemies. He remembered stories in history class about the famous trapper's war with the Crows. Johnson would rip out chunks of liver and devour them in front of the Crows he'd killed. The grisly scene that lay before him made it easier to believe. He'd seen skeletons, and he'd seen animals at every stage of decay, but never a rotting, half-eaten human corpse. The cannibalistic surrealism was overwhelming, and all feelings of control had long since departed. The thought of turning back was as terrifying as moving forward and only surpassed by the thought of staying still and doing nothing.

Wade continued forward, no longer stopping to inspect the carnage. He felt the press of the lair. He knew he needed to get his deer and get clear of the foul place without further daring its denizen. The carcasses and corpses no longer seemed out of place. It was Wade who didn't belong. The passage ended in another circular room similar to the alcove at the entrance. His deer was in the center, spread out like an offering at the altar of some dark deity. Wade flashed his light, canvassing the entire room. He was alone. He took off his pack and bent down by the deer. Teeth marks from the killer were visible where it had ripped into the flesh and underbelly. The heart and liver lay half-eaten in a heap off to the side. He grimaced at the wasted organs. His family ate heart and liver ceremonially after a kill. His fear and ire rose simultaneously. Another of the grotesque prints was visible next to the carcass, outlined in blood.

Aside from the organs and a couple of missing flesh chunks, Wade realized that most of the deer was intact. He felt the meat and made sure it was still cool. He maneuvered the deer so that he could keep an eye on the passage as he worked. His mind whirled as habit and instinct kicked in. He set about turning the deer into a backpack. It had already been gutted, so Wade wanted only to get the deer and bolt. He snapped off the back legs below the knee joint and made incisions between the tendon and upper-arm portion of its hind-quarters. He pulled the front legs of the deer through the incision, folded them, and used plastic zip ties from his pack to keep the contraption together. He'd turned the deer body into a pack with its legs as straps. Again Wade touched the necklace for courage. He stuffed his own pack into the deer's gut so that it couldn't fall out, as the opening would be sealed by his own back, and staggered to his feet.

The weight of the deer pack was light once Wade made his feet. He had done this before, and it had always been heavy, but terror and adrenaline propelled him and lessened the strain on his back. With his flashlight in his mouth, deer-pack on his back, and powder-rifle in his hands, Wade made his way back toward the entrance of the cave. His footfalls fell heavily onto the cave floor and crashed thunderously upon his ears. Each echo elicited a fear-filled cringe. A shadow halted him. It stood at the edge of the alcove shelf, blocking his way down. It was too far from his flashlight for Wade to make out anything but an outline, but it stood. Wade almost choked on the flashlight as he gulped. Something on two legs stood at the edge of his sanity. It was between him and the exit. It made to move toward him. Wade froze, but only momentarily. He leveled his rifle, cocked, and hip-shot in one fluid motion. The narrowness of the corridor and the closeness of his dark foe made it impossible to miss.

The concussion from the shot in the corridor of the cave was excruciating. Wade couldn't see where he hit, but he saw the creature stagger to a knee. It rolled aside and writhed down the other corridor, clutching at its side. Wade realized that he'd also stumbled to a knee during the encounter. His ears rang. Tinnitus made it impossible for him to hear anything. He felt a wet trickle on the sides of his neck and realized that blood was dripping from the side of his head. His ears were on fire, and his entire head pulsed like a heartbeat. He strained for footing and used his powder-rifle as a crutch to gain his feet. Wade sprinted forward to the edge of the shelf. He glanced to the side, raw droplets of blood splashed down the other corridor, their host not visible in the blackness. He dropped the deer pack down to the alcove floor and followed suit, not taking the time to scale the incline as before but baseball sliding to the bottom with his gun held high. The horrendous howl of the creature faintly penetrated the ringing in Wade's ears as the throbbing subsided. He didn't register how quickly he rolled over and stood with the deer pack until it was done. With his rifle in hand, Wade shouldered the deer pack and stepped out into the sun.

As Wade left the cave entrance behind, he was blasted with clean air. The shock of the cave's horrors compelled him to take flight, quickening his exodus. He checked the position of the sun as he ran. The weight of the deer and the tenuous footing bore Wade down. He glanced up as the sun vanished. Another weather front was moving in, and Wade knew he had to hurry. He stuffed his flashlight into his pocket, making sure it was off, unsure of his chances at making it back to the truck before dark. As the lair faded further behind him, the clutch of fear began to loosen. Wade slowed to a quick walk, trying to conserve some energy as he faltered through the snow. The weight bore him deeply into the ground layer, so he set the deer down. He reached into its cavity and retrieved snow shoes from his pack. He remembered that his gun was empty and pulled a speed loader out of his pocket. He poured powder down the barrel, placed a paper patch over it, and smashed a lead ball in with the ramrod. Wade tamped rapidly to make sure that the ball went all the way down and compacted on top of the powder. He took the spent cap off the gun's nipple and replaced it with a new one. He rose with the deer on his back and trudged through the snow.

Every step brought him closer to home, his muscles unclenched and Wade found a determined stride. He hoped the creature was dead. He glanced skyward, dark clouds had blotted out the sun, and Wade doubted that avenue of hope. He imagined the familial faces that would greet him if he made it home with the deer. The thought spurred him forward. More than any other aspect of hunting, Wade loved the awestruck look on the faces of his brother's children when he came home with a kill. They were always so animated and curious. They always screeched, "what'd you get, what'd you get?" Thoughts of not seeing their excitement strengthened Wade's resolve. He pressed on, too terrified not to keep moving. He was moving slowly, the weight of the deer sinking him too deeply into the snow, and he felt the sick anticipation of coming darkness. Wade had taken half the day to track the deer down, and even with his urgent steps it would take him longer to get back.

Darkness was falling. Wade knew he wouldn't make it back to the truck before the light faded. The thought of traversing the woods at night was terrifying, but hunkering down and waiting for the creature was worse. A tingling sensation in the back of his mind made him sure that the creature endured. Wade had to keep moving. His legs were faltering from the exertion, and his shoulders were on fire from the weight of the pack. He stopped, pitched the deer into the snow, and let his chest gulp in deep, barreling breaths. Wade had less than a mile to go but only a few minutes left of daylight, and it walking with the full weight of the deer on his back slowed him down. He reached into his pack and pulled out his emergency road flares.

Wade silently prayed and thanked his dad. His father had taught him to always pack flares. Sometimes it was too wet to start a fire traditionally; heavy snow or rain made flint useless, but flares always burnt. They were good for signaling help, not that any help was forthcoming. Wade stuffed two into his pocket and zip-tied another to the end of his rifle. He realized his ears were still ringing from the blast in the cave, and he knew in the dark he would be at a serious disadvantage. Unable to hear anything, Wade hoped at least to be able to stave off the dark.

He managed his feet again, sweat pouring off him and chilling his neck and back before it dripped down to the snow. He grunted forward, each exhausted step lifted out of desperation. As dusk set, the trees became threating. Wade imagined the windigo behind every branch, each limb an arm reaching for him, each set of branches a dangerously clawed hand. His flashlight only illuminated enough for him to keep from crashing into the trees. He wanted nothing more than to make a full-fledged dash to the truck, but the weight of the deer made running impossible, and taking deliberate steps allowed Wade to scan behind him for the beast.

As dusk turned to utter darkness, Wade struck his flare. The bright red penetrated the void in a circle around him. The light from the flare flickered and shade from the trees danced like movement in the brush. Wade cringed at each movement. Each reaching shadow filled Wade with fear. He held his gun up like a torch and marched forward, following the trail through the snow. He had fifteen minutes per flare, and Wade only had three of them. With ground to cover, his pace quickened. His heart thumped. Night fell.

The dried blood from his shattered ear drums served as an ever present propeller. Wade needed escape the forest. He trudged through the snow, waving his rifle like a sputtering, red wand. He noticed a log quivering in the distance, bouncing up and down like a springboard as it teetered above another log several feet off the ground. It didn't register immediately, then it struck Wade like a hammer, the realization behind the fallen tree's bobbing. Something had been standing on the log and leapt off, causing it to rock up and down like a teeter totter. He felt bile rise up in his throat, but he swallowed it back down. He had to keep going. He had to make the most of his flares.

Wade scanned in a circle, looking for his tormentor, but to no avail. Wade realized he was closer to the meadow than he'd realized. Hope. His blood-dried ears continued their eternal ringing, drowning out his own labored breathing as Wade moved forward, straining to hear something in the darkness. His heart fell as light vanished. The flare had died out. His eyes had grown accustomed to the bright red glow, and with the light removed, his sight had vanished. Wade fumbled in his pocket for another flare. His deafness terrified him, but his blindness was petrifying. The flare dropped into the snow as Wade struggled. He crashed to his knees with the deer on his back and stabbed the snow blindly. He whimpered as his shaking hands frantically searched the white powder before he grasped the flare by chance.

Wade struck the flare, the red flash as blinding as the darkness it expelled. He looked up and saw fresh blood on the trail in front of him. Clawed footprints zig-zagged mere feet away. Bile returned to Wade's mouth. Wade marred the white snow with yellow vomit. He realized that blood had dripped into the tracks as well. The windigo had stood there while he fumbled for the flare. It had watched. How close had it been? Then the tracks turned and followed the trail toward the meadow, leaving red splatters amidst their wake. The droplets continued with frequency alongside the tracks. Blood. Wade hadn't missed in the cave. It was wounded. Hope and fear mingled in his gut.

Wade realized he was only a few dozen yards from the creek. It felt like an eternal distance away, but he was emboldened by the windigo's blood. He donned his deer pack and headed for the creek. Wade held the flare in one hand and his rifle in the other. The flare was hot, but his cold hands did not register the pain. Wade realized the tracks were moving continually forward, and he cast aside any notion that the creature lay behind him. It lay in wait somewhere in the darkness ahead. Wade made the edge of the creek by the log and doubted his ability to cross it with the deer on his back. As he did the previous night, he decided to wade it. He jumped into the water, impervious to the cold liquid that splashed his legs. The sound of guttural huffing penetrated his perforated ears, and a violent shove from behind him sent him tumbling forward. He managed to keep hold of his rifle, but the flare flew from his hand toward the far bank. Wade crashed into the frigid waters. The cold jolted through him like electricity as he plummeted beneath the surface. The force of the shove jarred him from his snow shoes. The weight of the deer held him under. He rolled with the deer and pulled his rifle from the depths. Wade staggered to his feet on the other bank, his limbs sporadic from the bone-seeping chill.

Wade's eyes darted back and forth in dread. The feline predator smell had returned, as if the very presence of the creature offended the air. Wade whirled. It had crossed the creek while he was struggling in the water. On two legs, it stood at the edge of the meadow above him: a cannibal, a man-eater, the windigo. He could make out long head-hair swaying in the wind and short hair covering its limbs. Long, claw-like nails dangled from its hands and curled off its toes. He could just make out the edges of its bared, pointed teeth. Wade was unsure and afraid.

"Get back!" he shouted, but it didn't move.

Wade leveled his rifle, drew back the hammer, and pulled the rear trigger all in one motion. As he squeezed the front trigger, Wade saw its muscles tense. His heart fell with the hammer and the dry click of wet powder.

Illuminated in the red light of the flare that burned at Wade's feet, Wade watched the creature through a red haze. The weather had turned. Red-devil flakes fell from the sky, dancing in the light of the flare. Wade slowed his breathing. Get nervous after. He drew his pistol, still shivering from the icy waters. He fired.

Click.

The lack of percussion from the pistol was no surprise. He threw the deer from his back and drew the knife and tomahawk that his grandmother had given him. His knuckles were deathly white, both hands clenching the hilts of his weapons with a fervent grip.

The creature was stoic. One claw-like hand covered its stomach as its chest rose and fell with ease. The more Wade looked at it, the more certain he became that it had once been a man. Blood dripped generously from the hole in its stomach where Wade had shot it in the cave. It cascaded around hair-covered fingers. Wade watched as it pulled its blood-soaked hand up and licked. Its tongue traveled slowly, drinking its own blood. It smiled hungrily down at him, but Wade didn't avert his gaze.

They surged toward each other, Wade felt less the hunter than the hunted. He held his grandma's knife in his left hand and the tomahawk in his right. The windigo swung its razor claws in vicious, lateral swipes. Wade retreated, stepping back to avoid the swings. It cast both arms aside and yelled in guttural fury, again penetrating his damaged ears. Wade matched the ferocity with a yell of his own and swung the tomahawk hard as he stepped forward. It buried into the hip of the creature, eliciting a yell far less intimidating than its previous roar.

Wade didn't celebrate. The tomahawk sank so deeply into the hip that he couldn't loosen it. The creature swiped again, and Wade was too close to evade. Searing pain erupted from his own left hip as the claw ravaged him. Wade stepped back and watched as his own blood fell with that of the windigo. Steam rose from the snow where their warm blood mingled, adding to the reddish haze of the flare. Wade squared off again, refusing to give up. They circled each other again. Wade stood between the creature and his deer, standing protectively over his kill.

Wade watched as the flare dwindled. He knew the light was going to fade soon. His tormentor charged again, Wade unable to retreat for fear of tripping over the buck behind him. The light winked out. Wade closed his eyes and dropped to a knee, hoping the absence of red glare would be as blinding to the creature as it was to him. He felt the rush of air as a clawed hand swung over his head. Wade leapt forward, his arms extended, and he wrapped the creature's legs and lifted, driving it into the ground beneath him.

They smashed into the snow by the edge of the creek. Wade couldn't see in the dark, but he felt the warm, wet smack of coughed blood as air blasted from the windigo when they hit the ground. Wade blindly drove his knife into the windigo's side repeatedly. They roared together. Wade continued plunging his knife, battling through the searing pain that erupted on his chest, shoulders, and face. He realized the creature was clawing at him. Wade tried fending its arms off with his free hand as he continued to stab. Weakening limbs were swinging at him, whereas Wade's own rage boiled, increasing the strength of his plunges. He stabbed until he realized the creature was limp beneath him.

Wade panted with exertion. He pulled the final flare out of his pocket. Its striking red light emancipated the darkness. His chest pounded, his breath making red puffs all around him. Red streaks had turned to streams in the snow, covering the pristine white in an abysmal red. Wade huffed, straddling the windigo as he tried to regain his breath. He realized that his right eye was swollen shut, and his left side was bleeding steadily where it had first struck him. He took the flare and seared the cuts that bled the worst, screaming in agony and letting fall tears that were long overdue. Wade rose. He heard a whisper on the wind, the faint sound of his grandmother's voice. Wade looked down at the windigo in disgust and felt a terrible urge to burn it.

Wade gathered his gear. He made sure his pack was secured inside the deer's cavity. He left his shoes on the far bank, but picked up his rifle and pistol. He pulled the knife and tomahawk from the creature, sheathed them back on his belt, and looked down one last time. Wade thought it would have a pain-filled grimace carved on its face. Instead he found that haunting, familial smile. Somehow it looked relieved. Wade noticed a locket resting around its neck and chest. He ripped it from around the creature's neck and clenched it in his fist. Blood dripped from his white knuckled grip and fell in slow drops, further painting the snow.

Silent tears fell down his face as he took out his powder horn from his pack and poured gun powder over the body. He stuffed the flare into a gaping knife-hole in its chest. Red smoke spilled forth as the flare ignited the gunpowder, erupting into a searing blaze that devoured the windigo's flesh. Wade watched briefly as it smoldered, then shouldered the deer one last time and staggered back to his truck. He winced with each step and clutched at his side. He dropped the tail gate and rolled the deer into the back. The deer clung to his back, its blood having seeped through his clothes and dried all the way down his back to the crack of his pants. Wade was too exhausted to care. He pulled the pack from the deer's crevice and threw it into the passenger seat along with his rifle. Wade shivered as he let his truck warm up. He looked at his pale face in the mirror and winced at the gashes that marred it. The red glare from across the meadow dissipated as the flare died, but he could still see a faint orange glow where the corpse burnt. Wade clutched the locket as he drove away, wondering what he would say to his grandmother. He thought back to her stories the night before and the weapons she'd given him and realized that she must have known.

Wade followed his own tracks off the mountain.

I was born on July 13, 1991 and grew up near Crater Lake National Park in Southern Oregon. I'm graduating (class 2018') from Eastern Oregon University in La Grande, Oregon, with a Bachelors of Arts in English and a Bachelors of Arts in History with a minor in Native American Studies. I love the outdoors, hunting, fishing, hiking and any other means of discovering the wild places where people are scarce. My writing is both an expression of my experiences and an indulgence in my imagination.

AND LASTLY
AIDAN LAHZ

The helicopter seeds spiraled down from the shaded canopy of the forest and brushed delicately against Callum's arms and face as he trekked through the punishing underbrush. Scratching his legs as he went by, the bushes and ferns reached out in anguish at the beginning of their annual imperious dormancy. The air was so soaked that beads began to form on his skin and when he breathed, he was unsure whether or not he was actually drawing air.

He was confused as to why she asked to meet him in the middle of the forest. This better not be another one of her pointless expeditions, he thought to himself. She was always trying to find something to unearth, but she never did. It was always some else's shed, or cellar, or clearing. Never hers. His frustration along with it being incredibly hot that day was beginning to wear away at his morale. He had been walking for about an hour and still had no idea where he was going, so he took a moment to sit and rest. He sat and watched a single ant crawl up his leg, momentarily getting caught in a small streak of blood that had begun oozing from one of the innumerable cuts on his legs. He picked up a large, red leaf from the ground, and coaxed the ant onto it. He lowered it to the ground, letting it scamper away to the safety of the tree.

An amused voice called out from beside him, "Callum! I told you to follow the stream until you found me. I shouldn't have to go get you." He spun around to see his friend Simone. She slid her bare feet around the bottom of the stream that ran through the forest, sucking the refreshing chill up through her whole body.

"I got tired," he said getting to his feet. She gave him a disappointed look.

"Take off your shoes and get in here! We're almost there."

He slipped off his beaten up sneakers and dipped his sore feet into the cool creek. It pushed past him, sweeping away the pressing heat and cleaning the blood and sap from his calves. Rejuvenated, he followed Simone's beckoning gaze up the stream.

He could hear the rushing of the cascade long before it came into view. They rounded a bend in the stream and were met with the misty scent of spray as they neared the basin. The water flowed from a cave on the limestone cliffside, the mouth of which yawned like a petrified animal.

She turned to him. "Let's go! I've wanted to go find where the water starts for ages, but I was never brave enough to go alone." He chuckled.

They scaled the step-like indentations in the rock face to reach the mouth of the cave. A cool breeze rushed by them, sending a sickening chill through Callum's stomach. Simone reached into her backpack and pulled out two flashlights. She handed one to him. He took it and flicked it on with an echoing click. The walls of the cavern lit up, tinkling as drops of water rolled down the sinuous structures.

The stream flowed past them, growing less and less turbulent the further they traveled into the cliffside. The sounds of the forest faded away, replaced with only their dampened footsteps padding through the stream. Callum couldn't help but feel as if this gradual peacefulness was luring him into a false sense of relaxation. It was like the cave itself was willing them to go deeper, whispering in their ears and promising peace in the quiet darkness of its arms.

Simone scanned the walls of the cave, Running her beam over the lifeless expanse. Nothing moved but the water beneath her feet and Callum beside her.

She reached over and grasped Callum's hand, squeezing it tightly. Watching their step, Simone and Callum were drawn deeper into the cavern. It was hard to tell how far they had gone into the cliffside, or even how long they had been walking. Was it minutes? Hours? A day? The echoing of the cave became louder again.

"We must be close," Simone muttered, surprised by the fluttering in her voice and how loud it seemed.

Sure enough, the cave widened into a large circular crevice. Callum shined his flashlight around, staring in awe at the height of the ceiling, which loomed hundreds of feet above them. Water rushed down in sheets from all sides, pooling in the center of the room before flowing out through the passage they had just come through.

They hugged each other, focusing more on the tunnel that led back than the new place that was theirs. It felt taken, and private. It was like they were trespassing.

Simone panned her flashlight down from the ceiling, letting if fall over an undefined lump across the room. They glanced at each other, exchanging confused glances. Slowly they advanced towards the dark mass.

They stood only a few feet away from what looked like a cloth or a blanket, soaked and rotting with years of water flowing over it. Simone knelt down and reached her hand towards the cloth. The instant her hand brushed against its surface, it crumbled away, revealing a row of cracked ribs with a withered expression. The body was contorted in a disturbing, tortured position. The blinding shine from the flashlight off of the bleached skull surrounded Simone; her eyes filling with its triumphant laughter in her dooming curiosity. She screamed, scrambling back, splashing her back against the wall. It soaked her fear and sent it explosively throughout her whole body, radiating through the cavern. Callum's flashlight fell from his hand, shattering on the cave floor.

Simone's scream scattered across the cave, beginning again and again in an agonizing loop. The walls of the cavern shook, and boulders began to crash from above. The sheets of water turned into torrents as the walls crumbled away.

Callum raced to Simone's side, grabbing her hand and pulling her towards the exit.

"We have to go," he yelled over the crashing and churning.

Stumbling as fast as they could manage, they raced forward, the thought of daylight pulling them ever faster towards the cave entrance. The water rushed close behind them, growling and chasing them. Dodging the falling stones, their bare feet were cut by the sharp rocks that littered the floor. Simone's flashlight beam shook aimlessly around the cave as they ran. The water rushed past them, raising the level to their knees, tripping them up.

They struggled on, growing closer to the light of the mouth in the distance. Suddenly, a rock came crashing down, knocking Callum to the ground. Simone struggled back against the current to reach him. His leg was pinned to the cave floor. He screamed when she took his arms and tried to pull him out. Tears mixed with sweat and blood, and water.

"No. No. No."

A rumbling began in the distance. Simone's face filled with terror and desperation as the light from the cave entrance became scattered and then disappeared. The water pushed against the blocked cave door, and when it could not get through, it began to fill up the cave, fast. She frantically pulled at Callum's leg, but to no avail. He opened his mouth to say something but was choked as a large wave passed over his head. Simone held tightly to his hand, pulling until she too was swept away by a crashing wave. Her hand slipped from his. Letting go, she held him close.

Callum held his breath, his heart racing faster and faster, his lungs crying with frustration and despair. His eyes were dark blue with the rushing water. Simone's flashlight sat against a rock on the bottom of the stream, still shining. His heart, beating faster, then slower. Slow. Slow. A rock came crashing from the ceiling, shattering Simone's flashlight. Black.

Simone was spinning, disoriented as the vengeful river threw her off of cave walls and floors. Bashing. She reached out her hand and took hold of a crack in the wall, the water struggling to pull her away. She held tightly. A wave pushed her from below and she went racing towards the ceiling.

The water spat her out in a small alcove in the ceiling. Shaking and weak, she pulled herself to sit against the wall, hugging her knees, her head back in a sorrowful plea. Her wet hair stuck to her shoulders and neck, clinging tightly to her for safety. She breathed slowly.

Her lip quivered, and a fluttering sigh escaped her soul.

"I'm so sorry, Callum."

The water rose through the small hole in the alcove, running in tongues across the floor, licking her feet. She pushed herself against the wall. It coaxed her with its gurgling, and she slowly lowered her scraped and bleeding feet into the water. Sitting in it, she let it flow over her legs, higher. It picked her up gently as it flowed past her neck. Her feet left the floor and she floated up with the water, the pressure building in her head from the compressing of the air.

She reached up her hands to meet the fast-approaching ceiling. Pressing her lips to the stone, she drew one final breath and whispered triumphantly to the skull, the cave, the water, and to Callum, "One night awaits us all."

She sank beneath the water, floating weightlessly into the bright, beloved night. Her soul, free. Her body, bequeathed.

Aidan Lanz is a junior in high school. He lives in the Twin Cities, where he enjoys competitive diving and cooking. His favorite writer is Margaret Edson. This is his first publication.

LIKE AN OL ROCKIN' CHAIR
JAMES ANDREW DICKMAN

Your lungs wheeze and rattle like an ol rockin' chair,
Spring breezes brought a tickle than came a sneeze;
Staring into the abyss of this macabre nightmare.

Embracing you with coughing fits and causing your despair,
Gasping for your bony breath you sink down to your knees;
Your lungs wheeze and rattle like an ol rockin' chair.

Your skin crawls, and your pale lips clamor for air,
Your tight chest feels the big squeeze;
Staring into the abyss of this macabre nightmare.

With hollowed eyes and bluing nails, you've become aware,
That all life is ephemeral and by degrees;
Your lungs wheeze and rattle like an ol rockin' chair.

Feeling like you're drowning with a vacant stare,
Reaching for the surface can be such a tease;
Staring into the abyss of this macabre nightmare.

The Twilight entombs you in its lair,
And the Dark Angel you try to appease;
Your lungs wheeze and rattle like an ol rockin' chair;
Staring into the abyss of this macabre nightmare.

James Andrew Dickman, is an author and poet who delights in exposing the dark underbelly of modern American life with all its hypocrisies. For richer or poorer he is addicted to reading good books and poetry, and investigating what makes the human psyche tick. He has been featured in various publications including the SCBWI Bulletin Magazine, The Canyon Crier, the Writer's Newsletter (for poetry) and more.

I PAINTED MY FINGERNAILS WITH TOOTH ENAMEL
ELI ROWELL

let the bones clack together like the incisors
in my grandmother's skull, something like
a reprimand set in sharpness of her moon-white features, empty
eyes watching me tattoo another sentence onto my

ribs; this one is an addendum to the name
that I gave my last lover. The words start
out simple but transform into things other
because I can't bear to repeat myself

or it'll sound like I'm just reliving the same
few men and women that scarred badly, countless other
names that I'll never get to sink my tooth-enamel-nails
into, flesh tearing hair pulling lip shredding—

monstrosities I commit with broken-bone-fingers
that run over the skin of the newest name
I needle-pointed over my tenth rib just yesterday
morning, freshly woke and already your jaw

unhinged, curved fangs carving out hollows in my vertebrae
making it difficult for me to stand to walk to breathe
yet the black ink of your name still shimmers on
paper-thin skin, the only memory you'll

leave behind besides crescent moon scar on my hip

---

and a few crumpled dollar bills. They were never
going to be spent on me but I was wise to that
from the moment you took the first bite

*Eli Rowell lives in Tallahassee, where she is working towards a degree in
English while slush reading for a few different publications. She is from
Washington, D.C., and she sorely misses the cold summers (and colder
winters).*

BROKEN UMBRELLA
KATHRYN DE LEON

Silver skeleton by the sea,
unclaimed, forgotten,
lying in a grave of pebbles and sand.

Its black fabric
that unselfishly shielded heads
from rain and snow
lies beside it,
a shredded burial gown.
Its help is broken,
its work finished.

Someone will pick it up,
perhaps a child,
pull apart its shiny bones,
throw them at the sea,
then turn away.

The waves will take them in,
like God,
unconditionally, forgiving.

When I am broken,
will Death throw me at heaven,
then turn away?

Will God take me in
like the waves,

forgive me my selfish life,

the help I never gave
when I could have,
the work for others
left undone?

Kathryn de Leon has been writing poetry off and on since she was about nine years old, which is quite a long time! She lived most of her life in Los Angeles, but is now residing in England due to a life-long love of the Beatles. She teaches English in Japan several months a year, and also in England. She's had poems published in a number of small literary magazines.

THE BRIDE OF FRANKENSTEIN'S MONSTER, ON THE EVE OF HER WEDDING

LEAH C. STETSON

As I sit here on the brink of doom, upon a stool
Before a vanity of sorts, a cracked mirror reflects
My mutilated gaze, a ghostly vision, but no fool
I shall know joy, what he intended is circumspect.

First, I came 'alive,' or rather, electrified, but I won't
Argue the point; I could resist this lucky curse, instead
Rummage through my overnight bag, if I do, or don't
Deny it, either way I'll crush these fears or never wed.

Oh, these irksome tears free the grave-worms from my sockets
He draws me out like fluid from clouds, celestial, not unlike
My gift to him: a tiny glazed globe, which turns in his pockets
I literally gave him the world, and he navigated the Rhine!

What remedy of science unmingled this barbaric match?
Upon this, my wedding day, in these tortured environs,
Fixed as fate I will take him as he is, articulate wretch,
Who studies literature and writes essays in the dungeons,

Eloquent and persuasive, his magic eyes say it all to me.
I must now rehearse, unhallowed acts to be our vows;
A truce between duty and certain darkness, oddest dowry

He demanded a 'bride' and Dr. Frankenstein obliged, how

That mad-man soothes his creature's nightly nightmare cries,
Like a father to a child; I did not dream this, a life-mate of clay.
I'll promise to 'stay,' listen to complaints (a multitude of miseries)
Cling to his embrace and mend his bandages, soggy from decay.

Although loathsome, skin like lichen on a rock, he's not without
Softer traits, at least in moonlight, when it tricks the eye, a mirage;
His galvanized nature will sustain me, his wrinkled lips, no doubt
Will touch only mine, a constructed being, his little fiend-forage

Designed, the perfect revenge to accompany interchanged parts,
He shall be at once my greatest danger and unparalleled destiny;
We will leave this tower and travel with a gypsy entourage, start
A new world, our guests will toast to 'gods and monsters,' a litany

Of abominations put in better light. I've made a list, hypothetical
Terms of endearment—to sound them out on our honeymoon:
"Oh, unhappy dearest," and "My sorrowful love," or less trivial,
"Big debonaire daemon," which I learnt from Elizabeth, soon

To arrive and help me put on my dress, a tattered mess,
Stapled sail cloth from a fishing vessel (could she supply
Me not basic taffeta or gauzey-eyelet lace?) I have less
Than twelve hours to make do; if the gown be blue, my

Love is true. Another piece of wisdom from this pretty book
"For Brides-to-Be," I've gathered lily-of-the-valley to mask odors
Even though the author warns that the poisonous wood flowers
Repel men (the writer heeds, 'yet excites their seed') I will know

That soon enough! He will probably call me "Friend," and bleat

Perpetual notes, urging sympathy, not unworthy, possessed
With a dizzy sense of foreboding (the townsfolk, our retreat)
And bristle at relaxing until we reach a safe exile, our love-nest.

Are we bound for the 'land of mist and snow?' The alchemist forbid
Me hold a pen lest I record any such perverse account—thus, what
Could I do? And I, who cannot fathom a single line of letter to rid
My cousins' dread, since they already mourned my departure, sought

Peace. Yet, I must regain composure, brush these root-like tendrils,
Tangled as papery leaves, swirling in static whorls, Saturn's vortex:
A cosmic storm above my brow. I lean to inspect the fine, immortal
Lineaments—routes along a sentimental map that delineates my sex.

My gigantic groom will unveil me: uncommon mold, I will cool his
rage,
Endeavor to raise his spirits and tame that misunderstood nature,
imitate
His distinct species; I am neither his plaything nor idol of uncertain
age—
Oh, he spared me many hours of lonely degradation when he did
animate

The lifeless heart of this pre-determined woman! Instead of doing
harm,
He conjured hope, a dismal diamond in the rough, my divine rose
garden.
I will plant the bud in his pitchy mind: all my designs. I do not want to
alarm my king of spades, but I shall occupy my gangrene-thumbs with
that burden.

Surely my husband, even while he drives the sled, will come to
cherish

The level to which I stand, though not nearly to his stature, I persevere
In the harshest elements, yes, and I possess equal parts, will not perish,
But provide opinion and maintain autonomy of thought! I am clever.

Now that I've satisfied myself with reasonable intent to let
Myself be married, this balmy air revives me—sea urchins,
Sirens lull me into a forcible fantasy; I am utterly besotted.
Besides, with this hairstyle, he's the least of my concerns.

Leah C. Stetson writes poetry by the flash of frequent thunderstorms next to a Maine pond, a black ash seep, and a vortex. Her woods look like something from Chronicles of Narnia, or the setting of a Stephen King novella. Leah has taught English for Southern Maine Community College for ten years. Her writing has appeared in Wicked Alice, Arsenic Lobster, Omphalos, Red Ochre Lit, Off the Coast Literary Journal, Wolf Moon, Sea Stories: the Littoral Issue, LILA: Literature of Los Angeles, and New Maine Times. Her "Strange Wetlands" blog on WordPress was mentioned on Maine Public Radio. She holds a master's degree from College of the Atlantic, and is currently a graduate student in the Interdisciplinary PhD program at University of Maine studying the dark side of Romantic ecology.

WENT DEEP WEST INTO THE HORIZON SWEARING
GREG WOODS

Went deep west into the horizon swearing what I wouldn't repeat.
Sailors stewed and screwed never had what I captured there.
Where brown pelicans dare to wager wings to surf and eat.
Mercury and Venus cockeyed for good reason conspire.
Above black water brisk and indifferent awaiting the inevitable.

Taking helm to shepherd the noble from foregone conclusions.
Escaping what rhymes or echoes with the way this movie ends.
Away from ghosts blown back on rocks and shoals nobody knows.
Into darkness churning repeating curse words from way back.
Interspersed from top of throat with Hail Marys and The Lord's
Prayer.

Select pieces of the Post-Vatican Two Roman Catholic Mass.
In the California vernacular from memory for old times sake.
Holding tight with knuckles white from foam to bone shaking.
Blinking and leaping from foundation to conclusions written down.
Relegated to the confines of memory where lives are forgotten.

Greg Woods lives and works in Northern California, has published in Reed Magazine, California's Oldest Literary Journal, and featured as spoken word performer at the Austin International Poetry Festival. He currently teaches courses specific to Criminology, Criminal Justice and Legal Studies at San Jose State University. Additional biographical and contact information are available at the following: http://www.sjsu.edu/justicestudies/our-department/our-people/woods-g/index.html

I HAVE WHITE HANDS
NEAN HAWE

they fall upon my world like a soothsayer's
Doom
reeking of rot

bone White
protruding from fingertips

scrabbling at the coffin lid

ash White
the final ember
burns out

salt White
sown in my soul

nothing will ever grow

Nean Hawe is an aspiring novelist and poet from Salt Lake City, UT. He has a Bachelor's in Creative Writing from Westminster College and a love of dark tales and stark imagery.

DYING FOR IMMORTALITY
DIANE ROOT

"You realize," He said, managing somehow to look both benevolent and no-nonsense. "that you will have to die first before we can make you immortal." It's the kind of thing that would give anyone, save the feeble-minded, pause. The hesitation in her eyes prompted His reassurance. "Don't worry, it's entirely painless. You won't be aware of anything. You won't even be afraid."

"After all," He continued, "you are the last remaining mortal on this planet. Besides me" He added, smiling. That clinched it. She stretched out, closed her eyes and proffered her arm for the lethal injection.

***

The world had become so overpopulated, that something had to be done. The planet was decimated of sufficient crops, the seas nearly barren of fish, even the birds, now rare, could barely fly. Science, as always, came to the rescue. A new serum, painlessly injected, insured Eternal Life... to the "Chosen".

***

They weren't the only ones. Silence was the badge of honor among the ever-growing members of the Immortality Police—though that wasn't what they were called to their face. They wore their Immortality badge inscribed with that single magical word proudly. In bars and brothels, rest stops and restaurants, stores and shops, squares and stairs, cities and citadels, farms, fields and forts, ports and prairies—wherever there were people, all of whom greeted them with open arms. Here, they thought, were the walking, talking promise of paradise. No one in their right minds would refuse an offer of immortality, after all.

Of course, what they didn't know was that anyone not in their "right" minds would not be admitted through the future's earthly Pearly Gates.

The Project, as it was innocuously called, took astonishingly few years to accomplish, thanks to the legions of enforcers, all men and members of a tentacular and hidden society, sworn to secrecy on pain of death without the redemption of immortality. The Society, as they soon became known, spread far and wide as fast as wildfire. Their members were quickly and thoroughly indoctrinated by their youthful "elders," a quasi-military group of unusually handsome men, convinced that they were doing nothing less than purifying the species and creating Heaven on Earth. It was indeed a heady perfume to all that succumbed to its pervasive and an unperceived poisonous potion—a draught of delight devoid of deadly intent on their part, merely a desire to make the Earth a perfect place and its inhabitants a perfect people. Who, They thought, could disagree with such a noble cause?

It soon became apparent that virtually no one did.

***

Trillions had to be "treated". There was little protest: the lure of immortality overcame the fear of a "temporary death." They followed the "righteous" path like lemmings: Immortality forgave all, they thought, be it malfeasance or murder.

Besides, the ones who were chosen to be permanently dead wouldn't know of The Ultimate Decision, nor did they know that there was an alternative. After their demise, they certainly couldn't tell the living. Those who expressed doubts, mainly on the grounds of religion, were coerced.

Under this regime, pregnant women were euthanized; babies, supposedly immortalized, were killed in their cradles. Entire close families met a similar fate, but those deemed eligible, were brainwashed, so that they no longer harbored any memory of their offspring. After all, the Immortalists reasoned, what intelligent adult would want to care for a baby forever?

The same fate was allotted to all those below the age of reason, deemed to be at least 21. And even so, that unwitting majority, if judged unfit, met their doom without redemption. So were the ill and the old, the dense and the defective, the parasites and the paralyzed, the fearful and the ferocious, the religious and the rebellious. For that matter, rebels of any kind, likely to foment a revolution against the Society on what was considered spurious grounds–there were no non-spurious grounds–were also among the condemned. Imperfection would not be tolerated if it could not be eradicated by one means or another. The recalcitrant, of whom there were few, were told of a mysterious and deadly disease purportedly decimating whole districts of the unvaccinated, incurring unspeakable deaths. Once informed of the possibility of a terrible demise, the reluctant relented. The malevolent malady supposedly rampant was, of course, another fiction, promoted via means of the media, by now in the hands of the Immortalists. There came a time when resistance was nonexistent.

Not a moment too soon, as far as the Powers That Be were concerned. Saving the planet was primordial, overriding pity or compassion. Paradise was an undisputed primary goal. What's more, in Their view, there was no alternative. The Society's hemlock was a heady drink indeed, one of unrelenting power all in the name of perfecting an imperfect world. Intoxicating.

The doomed were led to their demise like lambs to slaughter. What's more, neither a whimper nor a wail was heard throughout the Realm.

***

In short, there was no way to escape the Immortality Police. Few even wanted to and those who originally rebelled were soon persuaded not to in view of the so-called plague about to descend upon them. Eventually, all subjected themselves willingly, convinced that they would escape the jaws of Purgatory or worse yet, Hell. Little did they know. Better that way, They said. What they didn't know wouldn't hurt them. Not at all, They said with a smile.

The "rejected" approached death with hope, similar to that of the ancient Egyptians, but without fear. Their souls would not be weighed in the balance of Fate, nor would they have to scale the hurdles along the highway to Heaven. They would not be lost in Limbo. Theirs would be a direct path back from whence they came. The Earthly heaven would embrace them. Once again.

Ignorance provided nothing less if not a merciful demise.

***

The "chosen" ones were either beautiful or handsome, brilliant, altruistic, generous, all endowed with just about any other wondrous attribute known to humanity. After the Immortal injection, they were excised of any and all faulty attributes, whether in their brains or their DNA. In short, they were perfect.

And uniform.

The Earth flourished. Tended carefully, the fields yielded, the brooks, rivers and seas were bountiful, the seasons beautiful. Nature's past anger with mankind apparently abated, the disasters of epic proportions disappeared. Wars were abolished, evil was eradicated, whether between nations or individuals. The planet was no longer Earth. It was Eden.

***

Not unlike the image of Henri Rousseau's painting, it became a Peaceable Kingdom. Man and beast, devoid of hunger or lethal intent, lived together, now nourished by plants that grew in abundance, cultivated by tireless hands. Lions and tigers, giraffes, goats, grasshoppers and iguanas, elephants and elands, bees and buffaloes, whales and wombats—all manner of creatures—lived and slept beside humans, since they, too, were immortal. The carnivorous became vegetarians, thanks to Immortalist engineering of DNA and the eradication of predatory instincts. Nothing that could devour, dismember, maim, mutilate, sting, or strike could do so any longer.

There were no longer any barriers. All things in this kingdom were woven in one cloth–kindness.

Fear and sin of any kind, of course, were unknown. Nor was courage. There was no need.

***

In this heavenly habitat, this paradise of plenitude and perfection, this plain of platitude, an unrelenting realm of an alternate reality, the estate of Eternity in which they lived, the Immortals became restless. Devoid of conflict or confrontation, battle or bereavement, guilt, greed, or grief, the Immortals were soon overcome by what the Good God Doctor had not anticipated.

Boredom. Ad infinitum.

Evil and the myriad scourges and sins of humanity had been abolished, but His joy of their eradication was soon eliminated as He beheld its ultimate outcome.

The Immortals, condemned to live forever, yearned to die.

Too late. Eternity has no end.

***

The Good God Doctor, the last mortal left standing, committed suicide as did His predecessors. The vial of Immortality serum, however, was found beside His body.

Unused.

To Him, Paradise had become a bleak and barren land.

Diane Root, a dual-national, was born in Paris of an American father, the journalist and writer, Waverley Root, and a French mother. Primarily known as a painter, she is, as she describes herself, "an accidental writer." She never sought to be published but that notwithstanding, she was nonetheless published in the New York Times Magazine ("The Artful Dodger" about lunch with Picasso) and various other venues. View her art: http://matakia.com.

BATTLING SKELETONS
JOHN GREY

On a graveyard battleground,
bones of death
rattle in immortal combat.
It's bone against bone,
skull crashing skull,
limbs flailing like tree boughs
in a hurricane.

Moonlight is skewered
by gravestones,
mausoleums of shadow.
Wind whispers prayers to the reaper,
cricket dirge mourns
the lost civility of the dead.

They fought when they were alive.
They scrap here in the afterlife.
It's a battle to the finish
that finished long ago.

John Grey is an Australian poet, US resident. Recently published in Chaffey Journal, Jelly Bucket and Columbia Review with work upcoming in Harpur Palate, Poetry East and Visions International.libraries across the U.S., and beyond. For details, please visit www.ronsinger.net.

THE SCAVENGER
CHRISTOPER ASLAN OVERFELT

Mouse's trailer is homemade, a rusted metal frame held together with crooked welds and broken bolts. At one point it had a wood floor and sides but the wood has long since rotted and fallen off. A single gray board hangs perilously on a bent nail.

Mouse, himself, has a bare frame with rotting pants held perilously on a single suspender. He crouches down on the frame of his trailer, across the spars of which lies a body. The body is clothed and Mouse begins by removing the boots and shirt and pants and trading them for his own.

Still crouching over the body, Mouse takes up a torch and strikes its nozzle alight, honing the flame to a sharp hissing blue. In the dark of night, the light flickers electrically as he begins at the chest and works the flame down the sternum and through the stomach. The skin sizzles as it separates in neat lines and Mouse shuts off the torch and begins to peel the skin from muscle and bone. He pulls on the long flaps and exposes the rib cage, the abdominal muscle and the organs below.

Taking a pipe wrench, he begins at the fine bones of the ribs and snaps them off one by one until he is able to break the chest plate into pieces and pull it apart. Below, the purple bulbous heart is harvested with tin snips, followed by the liver and kidneys and other precious organs. With a set of pliers, he detaches the eyeballs from their sockets and then moves to the teeth.

When Mouse is finished, the body is disassembled; the arms from their sockets, the fingers and toes twisted from the grip of joint and ligament. Even the fingernails are pulled and stacked in order from largest to smallest.

On the horizon in the east lies a sliver of light that is the same hue of the blue flame of the torch. The blue light gathers and emanates from the tassels of the corn that stand like rowed sentries across the empty land. Around Mouse is a pile of junk that has washed up into the corn like starfish on an ocean tide; parts of machines once honed and crafted to operate in perfect harmony are now discarded and cast off like members of a quarantined community.

Through the layers of junk, Mouse moves like a ghost, traveling through passageways with hardly a noise as he stores his harvest in crevices he will never find again. As the blue light dawns across the land, Mouse crouches with a handful of kernels and chews them one by one in his teeth until, in a nest of scrapped newspaper, he curls and digs his toes into the soft earth and sleeps.

Christopher Aslan Overfelt lives and works on the empty plains of Kansas. In the summertime he grows cucumbers and in the winters he takes attendance at the local high school.

HAIR: AN ELEGY
AMY LEBLANC

I.

You cut my hair with shears
and used the strands to thread socks
for the lingering months of winter.
I ran over a rabbit the next day.
She laid low beneath my tires,
her evening gloves stretched
up to her shoulders,
her tendons and bones
split like porcelain.
Her fur was matted like mine
with dirt up the back of her spine.
She bled in the shape
of a drowning thing.
I sat by the window
while the bees in our yard
pulled petals from flowers
to make perfumed wallpaper.

II.

The threads on my scalp
are like feathers in a bassinet.
I push strands down the drain
in the cracks of my chest
down the back of the couch
with braided crusts and breadcrumbs.
Without this fibril curtain

there is nothing left to cut.

III.

You told me my hair was strong,
which meant that I could grow
a body inside of my own.
You held a match to my hair
to see how brightly I would glow.

IV.

My mother said it's impolite
to die in a clean house.
I could imagine the shape of a body
sleeping on the kitchen tile,
hair splayed around her face
with freshly burnt coffee beans
grinding the floor below.
The floors had just been washed.
Her hair would smell like soap.

V.

I brushed my hair with the prongs
of a fork, not antlers or teeth
but they bit and they tore
the hair from my skin.
The candles were lit
with the flames in my ribs.
There is fleece from my underarms,
and lint between my legs.
Strings of floss fall down my neck.
The wick relents in a prescribed burn.

VI.

The bees flock to my hair
full of salt and honey.
I place my black strands on their hive.
we are the same them and I
we seek our mothers
to share tales of births and droughts.
I told the bees first
in their small petal hives.
Leave me not in my distress, I said.
I'll burn to stay alive.

VII.

Protein, keratin and dead cells
anchor each day into the next.
I don't have whiskers
to tell me when to run,
I have this nest in my head,
the flickering light
of oxidation against my headrest.
Hold a candle to the ends
And bleach me when you're done.
Seal me with wax
and dry me with honey.
The smell of wet wool
and the third week of winter
seep into my pores.
You sweep the ends into a pile
the size of a fist.

VIII.

The strands are specimens,
placed in a jar and drenched in chemicals
and cups of coffee.
The conservatory fills with vines
And grapes, clinging on their lines
Of thread, sewed together with hair.
They grow from my head
They seed to my skin
Pollinating and seething,
Trying to break free from
The killing jar.

IX.

You teach me how to pollinate
when I glow and I grow,
but I would slit my hair with an axe
before you got close.

Amy LeBlanc holds a BA (Hons) in English Literature and creative writing from the University of Calgary. She is currently non-fiction editor at filling Station magazine. Her work has appeared, or is scheduled to appear in Room, Prairie Fire, Contemporary Verse 2, and EVENT among others. Amy won the 2018 BrainStorm Poetry Contest for her poem 'Swell'. She is the author of two chapbooks, most recently "Ladybird, Ladybird" published with Anstruther Press in August 2018.

IT'S NIGHT (SUMMER)
KEVIN R. FARRELL, JR.

Skeletons out of the closet, strung together,
hanging from amber street lights,

bones hit concrete,
ghosts hover in windows,

rooftop movies,
melting into one.

Keep your breath bated,
you've got me hook, line and sinker.

Kevin R. Farrell, Jr. is an artist, poet, and educator whose work attempts to capture life from the vantage point of someone in the backseat of a stolen car running on fumes. His poems are a play on words in the form of political, satirical, surrealist, tongue in cheek rants that often border on stream of consciousness ramblings that are a last ditch effort at taking it all in before we get taken out.

For more information regarding Kevin's work please contact:
kfarrelljrart@gmail.com
http://kfarrelljrart.wixsite.com/kfarrelljrart
http://instagram.com/k.farrell_jr
FB: @kfarrelljr_art

HALLOWEEN POEM
LADY SAMANTHA

I wanted to write a Halloween poem
but I haven't the foggiest idea where to begin...

Do I start with the skeletons in my closet
who keep trying on my clothes?
How about the ghouls in my dresser drawers
throwing my underwear all over the place?
Or the the ghouls in the bathroom
who swim in and repeatedly flush the toilet?
How about the ghosts in the hallway
who call my name as I pass them?
Or the goblins in the kitchen
who keep nuking themselves in the microwave?
That is one mess I really don't want to clean up!
And don't forget those monsters under my bed–
they chat on their cell phones and keep me awake all night!
And what about the werewolf
who howls at the moon even after it sets?
And the vampire who's breath is worse than a period fart,
who sucks only his own blood,
and turns into a bat at 8 in the morning?
I question his motives.
Lastly, what about the jack-o-lantern with the creepy laugh?
Wait! I like him!
He laughs at all my jokes!

Lady Samantha is a writer and poet from Long Island, New York. Recent publications include Bard's Annual 2018 and Parody Magazine. Samantha writes poetry and short stories that would fit into many genres including, but not limited to, mystery, humor, science fiction, fantasy, and history.

THE SKY FLASHES WITH CROWS: A GREAT STORM APPROACHING
ALICIA MOONEY-FLYNT

Grandfather, a bent
man, spotted and rank with age,
explained once why the cat pawed
a mole for hours before killing it.
Its tricks bait the cat,
trapped by his swelling chest,
breathing in his gamy breath.

The memory hovers
and tears as the crows round
toward a scab of trees,
a cat lingering below.

Soon the sky clears to bone. My bones
shift and hum in the distance.

Alicia Mooney-Flynt currently lives, works, and dreams in North Carolina. Her poems have been read in Florida Humanities, Poet Lore, Shot Glass Journal online as well as others.

BONES
FELICIA CONNOLLY

i ache for your
scapula scraping
my neck as our cat
bodies slumber
thru the sick days.

i want the arrowheads
of your hips plunging
into mine while
the drive for sex dies.

at the end i'm
intimate with that
sunken cheek grin,
your xylophone made
of ribs.

it's so pristine,
this shell of you
i've learned to love:
your exoskeleton,
come to life.

Felicia Connolly, born and raised on the beaches of New England, now lives her best life in a small Texas town surrounded by sunshine, blue skies, and long grass. She spends her days baking and decorating cakes and her free time with her Rhodesian Ridgeback pup, Chewbarkka.

MOON RIVER AND ME
TAYLOR HOYT

For as long as I could remember, I was not real in this life. I slipped in and out with ease and without belonging.

My mother cried when they found me. I scrambled to understand why. I wasn't bloody or torn. Only purple and blue where panic collided on skin.

I remember my sister was always so funny. Jokes rolled off her tongue and filled the space around them. We made room, scooting back our plates, folding hands over our stomachs. Our laughter carried into every corner. Not even the dust mites could escape. I tried to copy that a power once; but, more interesting tales overturned mine and my words was lost, abandoned, and forgotten along the trail.

I saw him before. In the park, tugging a skinny retriever on a short, red leash. In aisle ten of our Safeway, trying to fix the squeak in the wheel. I offered to bring him a different cart.

My town was a smudge on a map. Pioneers on the way to Oregon lost who lost the will to reach that land of milk and honey. They decided that red dirt was fine enough, and so did their children and their children and theirs. I never saw anyone leave this town. I just saw it weigh on their shoulders. Every one of us was born in Saint Anthony's hospital and all buried in the cemetery. Ducks in a row.

Time is not a line. Time is not a scale to trace behind. Time is a record where the needle pulls itself wherever it wants along the grooves. There is no start. There is no end.

My father was the deputy. An old Air Force Staff Sergeant who handed every lesson with emphasis on principal. It was not just enough to follow rules. It was imperative to understand their reasons. Everything done, he said, needed intention. The basis of one's character always began with those bones. He made sure ours were strong.

My father called my mother Moon River. She styled her hair in that Hepburn way- her fringe sweeping across the brow, the ends flipped out no matter how much paste. She spoke french to me, mon lapin, and we imagined what the lilies would smell like down the streets on the Seine.

We blurred so quickly. The line between him and me nearly wiped clean. Soon, no one could hear my name without the conjuring of his face.

He was a man. He was one of us.

I was painfully shy. I never knew how to stand up straight, how to square my shoulders, or how to introduce myself. The only things that spoke to me in turn were my vinyls and cassettes. I drove forty minutes every other week to the record store. I would leave with a box full of migraines for my parents.

I never meant to hold my sister back. She always leapt forward, and I straggled behind on clumsy feet. We learned to swim together. She jumped into the marble pool with a squeal. She struggled to stay afloat, but she insisted on doing it alone. I refused to even put my feet inside. All I could imagine was sinking and sinking and the tile would open beneath me and I'd fall forever.

I was pushed into the water. My feet touched the floor. I didn't know how to reach the top. I sat motionless, paralyzed, my lungs burning and aching. My mother scooped me up and held me tight as I cried and coughed up chlorine and swore to never get in the water again. She said that was alright.

I don't know if he planned it. It was swift and sudden, an accidental violence. But the more I linger on it, the more I wonder if the intent was always there. I wonder if a snake coiled itself around his bones in strips of red and yellow and black. I wonder how long that snake waited with its tongue darting in and out.

My sister wanted me to go to a party with her. She opened the window latch and we crept through the yard.

My mother taught me how to crochet. How to get the stitches to pass from loop to loop. We copy patterns and looms. I contemplate this now more than before. I contemplate inevitability.

Was it always meant to be me?

"You're one of the Johnson's girls, right?"

I left the party before her. We were supposed to stay together. Always together. That's what mom said.

"It's pretty cold out tonight. I could give you a lift if you like. Wouldn't want you to get sick, right? Who else could bag my groceries like you?"

I could feel the heater outside the window. It smelled like vanilla and iron in there. My house was close. Fifteen minutes on foot, but easily five with a car. He was a little weird. So was I. I was different too. Maybe he just needed friends.

They would later recount this scene. Relive the choice none of them were there for. It was an uncomplicated moment to cherry pick. It was the easiest way to separate themselves from our shared possibility. Small town girls, they'd whisper in condescension.. Small town girls, still I would have known better. Maybe they would. But couldn't it have been anyone's daughter walking home that night?

Was it always meant to be me?

There were more roads than I remembered. I hoped I was imagining things. So tired I imagined the drive growing longer and longer. So tired I imagined the car slowing to a stop. He looked at me, calm eyes but sweat along his temple. The heater pumped the car to a stifling degree. I recommended turning it down.

My mother had lessons she feared we would never learn. She feared my sister would always be reckless. She thought one day she would wake to hear that funny girl joined some traveling band or drove the car through our school on a dare. Everyone joked about what a scene it would be to have the deputy arrest his own daughter.

For me, my mother feared I would never learn to use my voice. I let people talk over me. I let my words falter if the wind blew too loud.

When his hand lunged toward me, I screamed. My voice pierced the air like the crack of a whip.

They'll mention that too sometimes. If I was really the first, he may have gotten spooked. He just wanted a taste. Things got out of hand. He panicked. Were we just as scared, then? Were we terrified of what we were spiraling to become? Should I have screamed, mom?

I was upset at first when he threw me in the lake. My feet touched the floor. My arms did not reach to grasp that light from above. I thought about the stars blinking and looking over me. The water was deafening, beside the pull and drift along the shore. I watched the birds dart in and out for drink. I watched the moss collect around my skin. It was cold. It was calm too.

They found me. I do not know how long it took, but they found me.

My father pulled me out.

My funeral was the biggest in the town's history. There were cameras and reporters and everyone I had ever met. People from two towns over came with gifts and condolences. They talked and talked about how wonderful I was. They loved hearing my jokes. They always wanted me over. I brightened every room.

They quickly lost interest once they saw the closed casket.

Still, they all sang hymns. They cried with my father. They gave my sister flowers. They told my mother how beautiful she looked in her black dress.

He was there. He told her how sorry he was.

He shook her hand.

My room is how it always was. My bed is left ruffled in the corner. My shoes are lined against the door. Proof that I was here.

I see my dad more than I used to. They wouldn't let him work the case. They called it a conflict of interest.

My sister left. I don't know where she went, but it was far, far away. I hope she is happy. I am happy for her. My funny sister. My favorite friend.

My mother visits often. Late at night or early morning, she creeps inside my room and tip toes along the floor. She's always welcome. I watch her stand at the foot of my bed. She puts her hand on the blue comforter and spreads her palm across it, stretching the fabric. She smooths it out again.

She walks to my bookshelf, running her hand along the spines. She brushes off the dust collecting in the corner. It has no business settling there. Her eyes avoid the crate on the bottom shelf. I never thought my music was that bad.

It's been a long time since I've heard a tune. I beg her to play something, anything. I know they don't hear me. I wish they could. She turns from me, eyes focused on the door. Remembering gets hard. Memories turn sour too quickly now. I tell her I love her.

She stops halfway and I see the tension in her neck. Her fists close and open and close again. She turns back. I wonder if there's something she's forgotten.

Her feet walk toward the shelf. They are loud, even on the carpet. In one swift motion, she pulls out the box. There is a pause. Her fingers move slowly to the first cover's edge. She feels the flimsy cardboard, pushing back to the next record. There are so many options. I don't know what she looks for. I don't care which one she picks. I just pray she plays it.

She flips through cover after cover, searching and searching. Towards the end of the crate, buried behind so many others, she finds it. Her hands reach out and pull it up. She laughs. There is a triumph in her smile. I wonder how she even knew I had it.

She stands quickly, but when she finally meets the turntable, her hands shake. She cannot bring herself to play it.

I walk toward her. I place my hands above her own and feel her still. She lets out the breath I did not know she held in. She puts the needle down. The sound fills my room. It is warm and full and pure. It is everything and everyone I ever loved.

My mother lays on the bed with me. We listen while the notes swirl around us. She presses the cover against her chest. She closes her eyes.

Moon river, wider than a mile–

I'm crossing you in style some day–

I hold her close. At least, I hold her best I can. Her chest rises and falls. I hear her cry, but do not feel the tears hit my head, pressed against her cheek. She whispers to me. A harmonica vibrates across the wall. I track only the beat of my mother's heart. I close my eyes. I feel tired and warm.

Two drifters, off to see the world–

There's such a lot of world to see–

We're after the same rainbow's end, waitin' 'round the bend–

My huckleberry friend, moon river, and me.

Taylor Hoyt is an okay-ish person doing her best. She is a junior at the University of North Texas studying English. She hopes this might lead to a job someday (fingers crossed). In her spare time between work and school, she works on her poetry manuscript and short stories like these.

THE WINTER
ROXANNE HALPINE WARD

That winter crawled inside me
for warmth, took all mine away.
Even in May I still wore boots

and tights and sweaters, still
not able to believe in anything like
the spring. Even in May I was still

too tired to do more than work,
eat, sleep, work. I just kept
feeding that winter inside me,

not knowing how to yank it out
even as it gnawed my bones.

Roxanne Halpine Ward is a graduate of the MFA program at the University of North Carolina at Greensboro and a past attendee of the Bucknell Seminar for Younger Poets. Her work has appeared in the Georgia Review, Greensboro Review, and the Sow's Ear Poetry Review, among others, and my chapbook, This Electric Glow, was published by Seven Kitchens Press in 2012.

NARRATION / SOLITUDINARIAN / SLUMBERTIME STORIES / OUTSIDE ARTIST / EMPRISE
SANJEEV SETHI

NARRATION

We had the advantage of amplitude, our wing
beats could never choreograph their moves. It's
absurd to apportion blame to this or that. Signatures
on my codpiece were salutes to sand. No-one
remembers who left which doodle or dingbat.

Except for your arc. When most were siring I
was invested in your ecosystem. Some pitied
me for my predilections, those privy to my province
looked the other way. Which dominie could have
disentangled it? We took routes we thought
were right trusting hindsight to approbate them.

SOLITUDINARIAN

When your palm nudges me to its brace
it releases an assembly of motifs. Is this
dividend of my emotional stake?

In separation you are handy, closeness
places me in a psychological hinterland.

We have no secret except this one.

Gift of grief comes unannounced. It is a
dead letter but it reaches. Circumstances
roll their cuffs, nab me by the neck.

SLUMBERTIME STORIES

Sporting lodestar's daughter and dowager
both A-listers, were at a downtown gala
offering sound bites. The younger actress
spiritedly informed the house of how her
mother had metamorphosed to a dog lover.
"She lets her pup sleep on her bed." Was I
the only who noticed: tail-wagger has taken
the southpaw's place?

OUTSIDE ARTIST

Do intellectual accomplishments
of the aficionado matter? Or, is
a reader a reader? Venations prod
me to believe pathways unfurl.
Steer is to repurpose love and its
lure. Coziness of a cannonball
associates to before my time.
Disused emotions serve their scope:
essence relocates to craftship.

EMPRISE

Hesitancies played hooky when rapaciousness
overtook reasoning. I turned into a gofer of
greed. Chorus of breath garlanded my cravings.
Which is better: internal or external callus?
Profusion of philistines ensues fallout of the
artistic quotient. Palpable while at it in a bawdy-
house in another continent.

Sanjeev Sethi has published over 1200 poems in more than 25 countries. He is the author of three books of poetry. Wrappings in Bespoke is Winner of Full Fat Collection Competition-Deux organized by the Hedgehog Poetry Press UK. This is his fourth volume. It will be released in 2020. He lives in Mumbai, India.

MOTHER KNOWS BEST
KIMBERLY OWEN

For as long as I can remember, I've wanted to be like my mother. When I was a child, she'd always take the time to answer any question my budding imagination could dream up. Nothing was too much trouble for her and she never once made me feel like I was being a pain or getting on her nerves, even though, I'm pretty sure, there were countless times when this was the case.

She always smelled of cinnamon and apples. Her crumbles were the talk of the country fair and she always came first place, much to the chagrin of old Mrs. Eccles from number 72. How she hated coming second, but second was all anyone could ever hope to come to my mother. In my eyes, at least.

Her hair, soft and golden, fell almost to her waist and it tickled my belly whenever she dried me after my Sunday night baths. I'd laugh and gently push her hair away, but secretly I loved it. Her hands weren't soft in the same way as her hair. She spent too long with them in the hot dishwater or buried in the garden soil where she planted the most beautiful flowers for them to be soft, but I loved the rough texture of them when she stroked my cheek and told me what a good boy I'd been. I lived for those moments.

All through my childhood and long into my adult life, she helped anyone in need. She could never walk past a homeless person on the street, tears formed in her eyes whenever one of those adverts depicting starving children came on the television and more often than not, she'd reach for the phone and call the number on the screen. If a neighbour needed anything, my mother would be the first one on the street to offer it. No one had ever had a bone to pick with her, except maybe for Mrs. Eccles, and even then there'd be no malice. Mrs. Eccles just epitomised a sore loser. My mother, ever the rose-tinted spectacle wearer, laughed whenever Mrs. Eccles gave her a dirty look over the back fence.

If there's one thing I'll remember most fondly about my darling mother, who I always emulated and strived to be just like, it's the little phrases she had for every occasion. She had untold amounts just locked away waiting for the perfect opportunity to come out. If I left the door open behind me, I'd get the age-old, 'Were you born in a barn?' and if I left the room without turning the light off, 'It's like Blackpool illuminations in this house.' That one always made me giggle. Not to her face though. I've never been that silly.

My favourite saying of hers though was the one she trotted out whenever I didn't want to eat my vegetables – 'You are what you eat.' That's a good one, isn't it? You are what you eat. I hope she was telling the truth about that one because if she wasn't, I cooked her and ate her for nothing.

I've always wanted to be like my mother.

Kimberly Owen is a new author from Wales in the United Kingdom. Her stories have appeared in print magazines, as well as in online literary journals.

BONES
NINA BELEN ROBINS

I want to be
a mess
of bones.
Wrist bone,
vertebrae,
ankle nub,
clavicle.

You see,
if I reach to the
ceiling,
there is a rib cage.

The doctors told me
I don't need to lose more.
But the bones,
so smooth,
so elegant.

What am I if I don't
show them
off a little?

We hunt elephants
for their tusks.
lust for their ivory,
don't care that
they die after.

Smooth bones,
flawless bones,
priceless bones.

Don't you want
to see my bones?

Give me a glass
of ice water
and a salad,

and maybe
we can look at them
together.

Nina Belen Robins is a poet and grocery store employee. She lives with her husband and cats. She wrote the books of poems "Supermarket Diaries" and "A Bed with my Name on It" and can be found at Ninabelenrobins.com.

NO ONE IS COMING TO SAVE YOU / BLACK BOOTS / DEVILLED EGGS FOR MIDNIGHT SUPPER / FERTA, UNSETTLED 1959 / THE SKIN BETWEEN EGG AND SHELL / PHOSSY JAW / AUTOPSY / A HISTORY OF TOUCHING

ERIN EMILY ANN VANCE

NO ONE IS COMING TO SAVE YOU

It rained for five decades
and I hid in a tree house with a leaky roof
that my father built for my brother.
Outside, the youth were
a running puddle of sunless whales
where small jaws
are only built to cope
with the small bones of wild rabbits.

My geography,
the tar of my spine and the newspaper ink sweating
on the wooden floor.
When I ask the stuffed rabbit on the floor,
"Why?"
he tells me, "young bones that have not seen surgery
forget

and drown easily."

Green mold leaks out of his floppy ear.
I know that he is right, and I thumb the scar on my left elbow.

Three weeks later the rain stops and I emerge,
the rabbit tucked between my breasts,
I am fifty years and three weeks older
and I am the youngest person
still dry.

BLACK BOOTS

She perches on a stool in the kitchen.
A fat raven with legs too long and spidery
for her body.
She watches her mother ease the paper skin
off the onions, shedding the copper flakes
and the fragrant soil
onto the tile floor.
The little girl's black boots
are knocking, knocking, knocking
on the metal-framed stool,
its scaffolding a rusty skeleton
holding her suspended in the open warmth
of the bread oven.

Her mother comes at her with a small pair of scissors
that are rusted from sitting in the sink
shrieking like a dull axe or a golden scalpel
her mother places
a sliver of bay leaf on her forehead
ties

a butcher's knot into her boot laces

she takes the yellowed lace table cloth out of the closet
to ready the table
for Sunday Roast.

DEVILLED EGGS FOR MIDNIGHT SUPPER

When you sleep, she scoops your organs out
and places them in the blender with gold flakes
and dried rosemary
to starve the dreams of changelings.

With the precision of a homemaker at a church picnic
she whips the yolk of your being into peaks
and places sprigs of parsley on your dream-swept figure.

Upon waking with your body inside out
pluck out her right eye
and suck on the gelatinous orb
(she won't miss it, I promise)

Realize so much temper is in the instrument
and that she has to drag what fell
to the window ledge under the waning moon.

If she does not complain,
Let the mist of your steaming organs
slink over the marble threads of her bones

Stand in the throat of your floods,
your skin is a servant,
she is the breath you choke.

Ferta, Unsettled 1959

AFTER THE DERRYMAQUIRK WOMAN

In the mud, there are stories of women and foxes
and the yellow flowers that adorn their bodies.

Bring your bones to me, I say, and
with a flick of my tongue I will watch you fall

hold out your hand, I will read your fortune
with a flick of my wrist your wounds are packed with goldenrod

hold this leech to your cheek, your eyes grow wide
with a long suck I drain your abscess

In the mud, there are stories of women and foxes
and the yellow pus they drain from the bog cutters.

Languid, they heal and fell the men and the oaks
and sink back into the peat to tend to their infants.

The Skin Between Egg and Shell

Their bellies tear open like cantaloupe;
gaping splits in the cramped racket
of their breath.

Their empty bodies are broken windows
small teeth of jagged glass gnashing
at the passing crows.

The merrows are rough for their lovers,

their fingers are iron picks
that slip into the ears of unsuspecting men.

Meek-winged, they own the blood and drink
the well water, plucking a feather for each day
lost at sea.

They repel the moon like they are salt-whipped.

Below, the ground is plentiful. They find
syrup in each other like flies
and cry as if each tear had just been drawn,
a worm, ripe from the womb.

In elation, they sing with blood-filled hands
their skulls copper pots of plasma
spilling onto the flaxen dirt.

With morning come hymns to broken toes
and into the forest of the sea
they sink
with the flesh of sullen men on their lips.

PHOSSY JAW

"This match can be lit anywhere. Strike it on a book or the rough
wood of your kitchen table. Let the glow of the flame brighten those
dark London streets!"

I bought a frozen charlotte doll for my daughter, spent three days of
wages on a piece of porcelain in a matchbox bed.

The little matchstick girl died in the cold without a coat

but, did she glow, like me?

My daughter kept the doll beneath her head while she slept. I looked in on her, holding a chunk of my own flesh in my hand, my jaw a rotting socket.

She slept so peacefully, but the corner of my eye
Was a yellow light
that I couldn't quite catch.

AUTOPSY

The coroner reports from the anatomic findings and pertinent history that:
she had bad teeth
there was the smell of sex.

The police officer, brooding in the doorway:
"I must bring you an ugly piece of news"

Anatomic summary:
Bees lay dead in the after birth under the white duvet
Her prolapsed uterus was delivered last through the flesh

External examination:
The body is in a state of moderate decomposition.

She flushed the remnants of her womb and grabbed a bottle of apricot-scented hand sanitizer
She opened the cupboard where she stored the treats

Her fists grew bigger from bloating, the skin and hair sloughs easily with gentle pulling.

The gardener peeks through the window:
"What is that smell?"

Initial findings:
In the pea-green kitchen her thighs swell against a sharp elbow.
Her breasts plop out of her night gown,
swollen and leaking.
Possible scars from a lightning strike, unrelated.

An egg should never be boiled but she
had a secret desire to be sacrificed

Known history:
She birthed her first daughter in the basement
they got into furious fights and devoured each other, leaving only
their tails
The second daughter
she ground into the dirt of the planters like eggshells

Systemic and organ review:
To quell the smell of lingering afterbirth and decomposition, the lead
officer douses the body in strong coffee.

A History of Touching

They say a nun in fasting is crow-like,
mildest on her back.

Full like a gull with her chest to the sea
with salt-licked teeth,

a fasting nun is ashen, like a rocky-strewn shore

trapped long in herself like a spider,

crawling into muteness as ants do
and bloody as a beetroot
stolen
from the edge of the slow river.

The breasts of a nun in fasting
are mapped with blue veins that jut like bone matter,

shivering with hunger
or desire
or both.

Erin Emily Ann Vance's work is forthcoming in Coffin Bell Journal, Augur, Post Ghost Press, *and* Bad Nudes. *She is a contributing reader and writer for* Awkward Mermaid Literary Magazine. *A 2017 recipient of the Alberta Foundation for the Arts Young Artist Prize and a 2018 Finalist for the Alberta Magazine Awards in Fiction, she will complete her MA in Creative Writing in August 2018 and an MA in Folklore in 2020. Erin's debut novel,* Advice for Amateur Beekeepers and Taxidermists *will be published by Stonehouse Publishing in 2019.*
www.erinvance.ca
@erinemilyann (twitter, instagram)

IT'S SO MUCH NICER / IMMUTABLE / TECHNIQUE / MY FORMER LIVES
ROB PLATH

IT'S SO MUCH NICER

it's so much
nicer hanging
out w/ the dead
than the living
tongueless jaws
are better
vacant rib cages
are better
empty skulls
are better
horizontal frames
beneath layers
are better

IMMUTABLE

the skull laughs
when you try
to stifle it
its jaws happily
chattering
b/c it has no

tongue
to cut out

TECHNIQUE

i keep skinning
myself daily
& when that fucker
death knocks
it'll just be sickle
meeting goddam bone
the final poem

MY FORMER LIVES

i've never believed
in past lives
but thinking today
i've come to the conclusion
that i probably lived many
& i'm only in touch
w/ all those bones
of my former lives
a long line of skeletons
murmuring in my cells

Rob Plath is a 48-year-old poet from New York. He has published 21 books so far. . He is most known for his collection A BELLYFUL OF ANARCHY (epic rites press). He lives alone with his cat and stays out of trouble. See more of his work at www.robplath.com

MOON VIEW MOUNTAIN ROAD

FOSTER TRECOST

I once read a book of warnings. I can't remember the title, but it suggested cautions that should lead to a more leveled life, so I called it The Book of Warnings.

Our last night together was just like the first. We drove down the same road we'd come to know so well, a road we called Moon View Mountain Road. "Beautiful as ever," I said, but I spoke of the view, not of her [Do not lose beauty in everydayness, for to be surrounded by unnoticed beauty is to live in its absence]. She didn't respond, and I would have been surprised if she had.

We had found the road by accident. I'd been invited to a party, a Mountain Gala it was called. I could have taken anyone, but I chose someone I barely knew [Do not bring first dates to parties, for they deserve your full attention]. Since we didn't really know each other, we didn't know what to say, and we drove up the mountain in an uncomfortable silence. It was dark and the road unmarked, which made following directions difficult [Do not travel without a map, for it is better to lose yourself in those things you enjoy]. One wrong turn lead to another and we were lost long before we knew it. My embarrassment was worsened by her frustration, which seemed worsened by my embarrassment. When hope seemed just as lost as we were, the trees thinned to reveal a full moon rising from beyond the spruce. We each broke the silence with a gasp, and then let it return, but it was no longer uncomfortable.

We never made it to the Gala, and I was never invited to another [Do not break your commitments, for those expecting you may not be the next time], but to Moon View Mountain Road we returned many times. That was many moons ago.

I said again: "Beautiful as ever." The thin mountain air allowed for an even brighter luminance. As a child I thought the mountain moon was brighter because we were closer to it. I miss the innocence of those days [Do not grow up, for a child inside will keep you young on the outside]. I looked at her, moonlight pulling the tips of her fragile face from darkness. She did not smile. Her eyes were closed.

In better times we would drive Moon View Mountain Road, but not lately. She had become bored with me, but found it easier to say she had become bored with the moon. We stopped talking [Do not speak with your silence, for it will say things unintended]. We stopped everything. Earlier that day, I pleaded for her return and suggested we take a drive. "The moon can't save us now," she said.

"But it can," I pleaded. "It can show us who we used to be," but we both knew the moonlight would reveal nothing more than a man she used to love. "Would you rather he took you?" [Do not ask questions unless you are prepared for the answers, for the truth often hurts].

"Yes," she said.

I had woken to a hopeful day. In the morning I planted rose vines along the back trellis, weaving them through the diamond-shaped pattern. I then repaired a loose shingle near the chimney, wanting it fixed before the spring rains. After lunch, I busied myself with yard work.

"Yes," she said.

"We're almost there," I said, but I wasn't in a hurry. Neither was she [Do not kill people, for to end another life is to end part of your own]. I pulled to the side of the road and turned off the engine. I carried her body to the edge of a clearing with no trees to hide the moon. I looked at the moon that would forever rise above her. "You're right," I said. "It can't save us now."

I covered her and waited for remorse [Do not have regrets, for to live with lament is not to live]. She's only bones by now, and I'm still waiting.

Foster Trecost writes stories that are mostly made up. They tend to follow his attention span: sometimes short, sometimes very short. Recent work has appeared in New World Writing, Star 82 Review, and Speak Fiction. He lives in New Orleans with his wife and dog.

DYING WITH GRACE
R. M. SCHNEIDER

On Sundays, around 2pm, dinner would be ready and spread out on the kitchen table. It usually consisted of a hunk of meat, bleached white sandwich bread, a canned vegetable, and salad from a bag. If we were lucky there would be mashed potatoes, and they would be fresh instead of made from those instant flakes that come in a box. Those kinds always reminded me of dandruff and made me lose my appetite.

Around that time, I was usually in the living room sinking into one of the lazy boy chairs, letting the television brainwash me to sleep. Then the clock on the wall next to me would chime out on the hour, and one or two of my uncles walked through the front door, and I never looked to see who it was because it was always the usual suspects. Dishes and silverware would start clanking and scraping, and sometimes one of them would come over and sit in the second lazy boy with their plate, maybe stay for a few minutes after they've finished, and then a few more minutes later the front door would open again, and everyone would leave.

Most Sundays it was like clockwork, but there were also some odd days when no one would show up. Dinner would be spread out on the table, all the lights in the house would be off, and the clock would tick on while the food got cold and dusty. My grandmother, Grace, always made the food but rarely ate herself. When she was done cooking she would shuffle over into the living room, plop herself down on the couch, and light a cigarette, expecting everyone to fend for themselves.

Eventually, she would fall asleep, and I'd go into the kitchen and make a plate for myself. I left the lights off, letting only the natural light streaming in through the windows show me what I was eating.

The silence and the tick of the clock surrounded me as I sat at the table alone.

When I was done I put my plate in the sink and went to stand by the kitchen window. Outside it was bright, but from inside it looked like a bleak summer day, like if you went outside you'd feel like you were stranded in the desert. Grace never left the house, and it often felt like I couldn't myself. I'd walk around the house and peer out each window like they were exhibits in a museum. I'd look out at the big world and up at the big sun, watching it look down at me, so small in comparison like I was the one in the museum but didn't know it. I'd often forget the hold her house had on me, and when I remembered again I would decide to leave for a while to get away from such obscure thoughts.

I'd walk through the yard, observing her nearly empty garden, which only had a couple of rose plants in it. They were covered in thorns and only bloomed one blossom at a time; when one would die only then would another take its place. I watered them and continued to walk around to the back of the house where there once used to be a cherry tree and more grass, but now there was only an empty lot of gravel.

I'd only heard stories of the tree and some of the fond memories the family had of it. It was cut down before I was born, but even still, seeing nothing in its place day after day saddened me, as if I had memories of it too. Maybe I used to climb it and swing from the branches. Maybe in the spring when it bloomed I would fall asleep under its shade and dream. I would look up and ask it to watch over me while my unconsciousness swam around in pools of possibilities. Its blossoms would fall softly like snow and cover me, maybe as its way of protecting me.

In the summer when the fruit would begin to ripen, the children would take turns picking them off the tree. One would hold the ladder, and the other would pick. Grace would watch through the kitchen window, while her husband stood in the yard watching with his hands on his hips. There would be fighting and laughter, and afterward, the girls would help their mother make cherry pie.

When I asked Grace about the tree she would just say something distantly like "That was a nice tree...," and nothing more. She didn't like to talk about it. The tone of her voice would change, and she averted her eyes away from me or whoever was prying.

I could taste and smell the cherry pies in my daydreams, while I stood in the middle of the lot and kicked around the small stones as if they were the bones of all the fallen fruit.

After a while, I would make my way back inside and continue to watch over her, and after a while longer Sunday would be over and my Mother would arrive to take me home. I'd hug Grace goodbye and wait for the next Sunday to come.

In the mornings I woke to the sight of yellow floral wallpaper, and after a few groggy blinks, I realized I was in her bed and it was Sunday once again. She was already awake, shuffling around the kitchen, back and forth, from the coffee pot to the newspaper spread out on the kitchen table. I would continue to lie in bed, wondering how long she expected me to sleep.

Eventually, I too made my way into the kitchen, when the daylight became too hard to ignore. I sat down at the table and stayed quiet like I was still sleeping. I watched her scan the paper like she was searching for something, reading the obituaries like everyday news, holding down the edges with both hands, and then she would pause and shuffle over to the coffee pot to fill her cup and back again, never once sitting down. I assumed it was just easier to flip the pages that way.

In her cup, decaf, with lots of cream and sugar, the opposite of how I took my coffee. Just thinking about the amount of sweetness and lack of caffeine made me cringe and her restlessness made me anxious, so I headed into the living room to watch TV.

The whole house filled with light as I let the TV brainwash me into mindlessness. In that state, every hour began to seem like it was only minutes away, then seconds, and then the clock would chime out in eight consecutive tones. After a while, she would also shift into the living room, plop down on the couch, turn on her shows, and light a cigarette. I would get up once and a while and shuffle around myself, stretching my legs as to not become part of the furniture.

Besides the clock ticking and the chatter of the television, the house would be quiet for hours. We had one of those things where you didn't need to say much to know each other well. You didn't have to say anything at all. You just sit there together comfortably in silence, not saying a word for hours on end. A mumble and shuffle here, comments on the TV program there, giving the answers to Jeopardy, and expressing subtle disgust towards the news.

Occasionally some of her children would come and go, no need to knock, no need to say goodbye, come as you like, do as you please, just don't wake Grace up from her nap, and don't disturb her routine because it's still her house. It's her lovely dollhouse that she let others enter and mill about in. It was hard not to take it for granted.

One afternoon, we were halfway through our Sunday routine. I sat in the lazy boy, and she shuffled around in the kitchen. The TV had already put me to sleep, and I was becoming part of the furniture, sinking into it like quicksand. The slam of the door woke me suddenly, and for once I turned my head to see who it was. It was one of the usual suspects, my uncle, and he was running over to Grace, who had collapsed on the floor. I pulled myself out of the quicksand consuming me and ran over to her too.

While everything seemed to progress in slow motion, my uncle called 911, and some of the other family members. My heart raced, and it was all I could hear in my head as I helped her into a chair, her gripping her chest. Then my ears began to ring. Suddenly any memories I had begun to pulse away from me, and with each heartbeat, I was becoming further and further away, while her frail bony hands squeezed mine.

A few minutes later we could hear the sirens approaching from the distance until they were blaring right outside. My uncle flung the door open and two men in clean white uniforms ran in and took her away, leaving us feeling useless. And after that everything went blank.

Later that day we all sat in the hospital room. The beep of the monitor and its consecutiveness drew my mind back to the tick of the clock. When she came around, we were there to greet her and ease the fear she had just met — the fear of death. Then she turned to me, looked me in the eyes, and asked where I was when she called my name time after time to come to her aid. I didn't have an answer, because the guilt had already begun to eat me alive. Saying the words "I didn't hear you," to her would have broken every heart in that room, including mine. Instead of answering I just choked up an "I'm sorry," and again felt her frail bony hands squeezing mine. The rings on all her fingers left bruises.

During the days she was kept there the flowers in her room kept adding up as word spread to extended family and friends. I visited every day along with many others. I sat next to her as she slept, and when she was awake I read her the notes that came with the flowers. At one point she told me to stop and turn on the TV for her instead.

"I've heard enough of that. I don't like all this attention. Can you turn on my shows?"

I stared at her and then up at the TV with sadness and went over to turn it on. The thought of having the TV on now put a pit in my stomach.

It was time for Jeopardy. I watched her as she watched the show and answered the trivia questions aloud, and just then I remembered it was Sunday. It had been a week and I didn't even notice. I looked out the hospital window and out at the sunny day that looked bleak from inside. The lights in her room were off and filled with the same kind of afternoon shadows that would be in her house at that time of day. Then the TV went to a commercial break and began advertising products directed towards people like her.

"Did you get to read the paper this morning?" I asked her.

"I did, but the pages are hard to flip sitting in this bed. And Margret Hughes died," she said without taking her eyes off the TV, and without emotion.

"Didn't she live somewhere in the neighborhood?"

"A couple streets over from us, and she only sat a few pews over from me in church," she said still glued to the screen.

"Grace it's time for your medicine," announced the nurse as she walked in with a small white paper cup in her hand and a glass of water in the other.

"Can I have some coffee to wash it down with?"

"No, I'm afraid not, the doctor doesn't want you drinking any coffee, but I brought some refreshing water for you."

"Not even decaf?"

"I'm afraid not."

She looked at the smiling nurse blankly and took the water and pills from her hand. Then she showed the nurse the inside of her mouth and the bottom of her tongue to prove she swallowed them.

"This is more like a prison," she grumbled when the nurse finally left the room. It was clear and not surprising that she was frustrated she couldn't do everything in her usual routine. None of us liked change.

An hour or so later, after she woke from her nap and started watching the news, my mother showed up to take me home. I wanted to insist I stay and watch over her a while longer, but I knew me leaving at the same time every Sunday was part of her routine too.

Outside the daylight was bleak like it seemed it would be from inside. As I walked through the parking lot I could feel the heat of the sun weighing me down. I could tell it was watching me, like a giant eye in the sky. Each day going to and from the hospital was never-ending and exhausting. Only one day did it rain; the sky was dark, and her room really did feel like a prison.

When they allowed her to leave the hospital and return home she was relieved as anyone would be. She could finally and properly get back to her routine. We helped her out of the car, up the steps, and through the door of her home. Everything was the same as it had been. The chair I helped her into was still pulled out from the table, and as she shuffled passed she pushed it back into place. The TV in the living room was still buzzing, and I swiftly walked over to turn it off, while she stood at the counter and made a fresh pot of coffee.

The following Sunday I woke to the yellow floral wallpaper and laid in bed for a while staring at the ceiling. The days had seemingly gone back to the way they were, but I was changed now. Eventually, I got out of bed and made my way into the kitchen to sit down at the table, but as I did I noticed I couldn't because she was already sitting in my chair. The newspaper was open, and her coffee cup was empty.

"Laura dear, can you fill up my cup?" she asked a bit embarrassed, and so I did and sat down next to her while she continued to read the paper. It was quieter than usual, even though we didn't talk much, to begin with. Now our minds were quiet too, empty and troubled, not sure what to think or do. The rest of the day was like that, and at one point she crawled back into bed.

At 2pm the clock chimed out like it did, and none of the usual suspects came barging in through the door to see what was for dinner because there was none. I stood alone in the kitchen with all the lights off, buttering a piece of toast.

Every Sunday after that became slower and quieter, until one day I arrived a Saturday afternoon and she was nowhere to be found. I searched the entire house, but there was nothing but empty rooms and darkness filling them. I sat down in the living room and waited awhile. I left the TV off, and it began to mock me as I stared into the black mirror-like screen, surrounded by the silence and ticking. There was a sickening feeling in the dry smoky air. My reflection looked concerned and was trying to tell me that something was wrong. I sat still while she motioned something to me from the other side of the screen.

Later that evening, the door opened and startled me awake, and my Uncle walked in with Grace's arm in her hand, helping her shuffle along. She could no longer walk for herself, along with many other things, and according to the doctors we had to start treating her like the stroke victim she was, and the cancer patient we would soon discover her to be.

The Sundays, the dinners, and routines had disappeared, and were replaced by busy bodies tending to her every need. Instead of coffee they gave her health shakes and Jell-O, and the pills were endless, one of every color and size, just like she was back at the hospital. It seemed the prison had been brought back to her home and had her trapped again. She sat at the kitchen table speechless and saddened as the days passed her by. She would sigh shortly, rub her boney hands, and stare at all her rings. Each one on each of her fingers represented a different memory, and so she reminisced.

Sometimes I would slip her coffee and cigarettes when no one was looking. She desperately wanted her humanity back, and it didn't take long for her to become hopeless. She spent hours sitting, staring at the walls, staring at her rings, and staring at the paper. I would often sit and stare with her and flip the pages of her paper. She no longer seemed eager to search, for whatever it was. She pushed away the paper when she got to the obituaries, because maybe she was afraid that what she would find would end up being herself, staring back up at her, alongside Margret Hughes. She sighed and pictured all the empty church pews that kept adding up.

The end of summer arrived suddenly. It snuck up on me and consumed the whole town in heat and anticipation. I knew I had to leave for school soon, I had already packed, and so I also knew I had to say goodbye, for now, to Grace, and to everyone.

At the last moment of the last Sunday I got up from my seat next to her at the table when my mother beeped the car horn and told her I'd see her soon. I tried to leave her with a smile, but she didn't look at me to see it, and then quiet tears began to stream down her face. I put my hand on her shoulder for a moment, and then left out the front door.

A couple days later she passed away. Constantly the image of her crying face appeared in my mind like a bad dream for many days after. No one had ever seen her cry, I realized, and at the time I should have seen that the hopelessness in her mind had been replaced with more fear and that she knew it would be our last goodbye.

When I returned home for the funeral, I also returned to the house. I could already see the color in everything beginning to fade, and the shadows getting ready to take their place and fill up all the emptiness left behind. I sat in my lazy boy chair and waited for the clock to chime out and break the silence. It was four in the afternoon, and I was the only one in the house. Everything was still untouched, and the dust and the pictures it clung to still hung on the walls. All the objects in the house were staring at me. My reflection in the TV screen still mocked me. I looked over at her seat on the couch, and then reclined to the fullest the chair would allow, feet up and all, so I was staring up at the ceiling and the cobwebs in its corners. When I closed my eyes, I could picture a time lapse of all the dust piling up on the furniture, and the wallpaper turning yellower and starting to peel off. Eventually, the shadows would consume everything, and the house would disappear.

Later, as I stood in the cemetery draped in black, I pictured a different time lapse of the dirt piling up on her casket, until she was deep underground. Up above the seasons went by and grass began to grow until it was tall, and then someone came by to mow it. When winter came there was a blizzard and the snow piled up until she was buried even deeper. Spring sped into summer and the grass began to grow again. Each day it got hotter and hotter until the grass brown, and the flesh began to melt off her bones.

Meanwhile, I was stranded somewhere in the desert trying to escape the blazing sun and the endless sweltering days. I crossed it with my feet dragging in the sand, pulling myself along with no end in sight, and it soon turned to quicksand and began to consume me. The eye in the sky watched me with sickening pleasure when the heat began to get to me and burn my skin. I dropped to my hands and knees and began to crawl away from the vultures that had begun to circle high in the sky above. They could see me dying slowly and were getting eager to pick at my flesh before the heat melted it off my own bones. Then autumn sped by and winter returned.

As the years passed, whenever I returned home again I found myself standing in her kitchen. All the lights in the house were off, and light streamed in through the windows while the clock continued to tick on, just like one of those Sundays. No one lived there anymore, and no one came by after she passed away. But I still had a habit of wandering through the house and peering out the windows. I watered her roses and thought longingly about the cherry tree.

Then after a while, I would return to the house to watch over the place she used to sit. I sat in the lazy boy, looking around at all the strange silence and the dust particles floating about in the slivers of light while suffocating in the stale smoky air. I did so until the late afternoon was creeping up on me, and the shadows were beginning to set in. They now hung on the walls like all the framed memories and pieces of art that now collected even more dust, as if someone put her dollhouse in the attic, and with me, the only one left inside. Everything was already in motion, and her memory was already set to fade away.

And even when I left and no longer returned, and the house no longer existed, I was still stuck there with her memories and her lingering ghost. I'd go through the rest of my days, finding myself in strange places, and suddenly I'd hear a clock chime out. I'd look at my watch and expected it to read 2pm.

R. M. Schneider is a dance teacher and fiction writer living in Pittsburgh, Pennsylvania.

BONED / BACK-FLIP MOVE / MAN-DOG DOUBLE BECOMING
M. A. ISTVAN, JR.

BONED

what is the true target of our rage
when we rage at the dog gnawing in bliss
on the dug-up bones of a loved one?

the slow formation of the belief that abuse
does not count as abuse when abusing
those without the backbone to stop it

an audible crack as the tailbone fractures in childbirth

cocks fighting for microwaved boneless chicken wings

let bones, ligaments, tendons
take the weight
of the shoulders

are those who value effort over outcome
prone to feel less alive if what they use—
shoes, drums, bones—never wears out?

that elephantine need to stroke the bones of your own kind

------

transwomen scrutinized
for having the right features:
bone structure, voice, facial hair

undernourished enough to feel your backbone through your stomach

BACK-FLIP MOVE

I see my cousin only at rare family get-togethers.
He does that same breakdance move each time.
Arms out like Christ, he falls back, budgeless
in a back-flop. This last wedding I asked him
if he was still b-boying. He said he keeps it up
a bit, despite bone issues from so many years.

At the reception, he was popping and locking
by himself at first. But as his demand for space
increased with his flails, a cheer circle formed
around him. I had forgotten his black-flop move,
which he ends his show with and does only once
per get-together, until he pulled it out that night.

If I felt cringey seeing this, then I wonder how
his close family felt. How does he bring himself
to do it with them watching? They know right
when it will come. Am I just projecting? Might
they be eager for the cheers, eager to see others
see the talent of their son, grandson, nephew?

MAN-DOG DOUBLE BECOMING

Restricted from venting instinctual caprices
in his deprived state of caution and hesitation,
the dog nibbles bald patches into himself:
taming himself, beating back brute instincts
no longer adaptive, lacerating himself
to accept the strictures of his situation,
crafting a micro-soul that finds anesthesia
and even pleasure in such inward cruelty—

a soul that has him look down and whimper
(in perverse pleasure, it seems) if by chance
a growl still manages to escape his throat.
And man too self-ravages himself, not just
by crafting an even richer inner world—
a soul—of guilt, but also by nibbling himself:
flaying skin, wearing down bone, after years
to a state as awful as the bald spots in the fur.

M. A. Istvan Jr., PhD is known to warp the subjective tapestries of those in his vicinity. Almost everyone who comes into his ever-emanating distortion field will inadvertently take on his reality (his values and goals), finding within themselves a heightened sense of potential where old excuses for not going for the brass ring slip away. Not wanting to feel the spur to evolve, most avoid him out of the same gut instinct that has them avoid meditating yogis and sustained eye contact even with family. Those who do enter his field run the risk of becoming addicted to being at his side. Istvan's personal challenge has always been to push them from the den, not only so that they may grow on their own.

BONED: A Collection of Skeletal Writings is a project started by Nate Ragolia in 2016. Each Tuesday, a new story, poem, play, or essay posts. The common theme is that all content features either bones, or a skeleton, in some capacity.

Read each week at bonedstories.wordpress.com,

ABOUT THE PUBLISHING TEAM

Nate Ragolia was labeled "weird" early in school, and it stuck. He's a lifelong lover of science fiction, and a nerd/geek. In 2015 his first book, *There You Feel Free*, was published by 1888's Black Hill Press. He's also the author of *The Retroactivist*, published by Spaceboy Books. He founded and edits BONED, an online literary magazine, has created webcomics, and writes whenever he's not playing video games or petting dogs.

Shaunn Grulkowski has been compared to Warren Ellis and Phillip K. Dick and was once described as what a baby conceived by Kurt Vonnegut and Margaret Atwood would turn out to be. He's at least the fifth best Slavic-Latino-American sci-fi writer in the Baltimore metro area. He's the author of *Retcontinuum,* and the editor of *A Stalled Ox* and *The Goldfish,* all for 1888/Black Hill Press.

Antoine Valot, Graphics Bot is a 2015 Nexus™ series Replicant from the Tyrell Corporation, communications/design model. He enjoys designing book covers, nitpicking about words, functioning within his operating margins, and making the most of the two years he has left to live.

Learn more about Spaceboy Books at readspaceboy.com

This book features the font Skullphabet by Noah Scalin (Skull-A-Day). Learn more about Skull-A-Day at skulladay.blogspot.com